THE ROUGH GUIDE TO
NORTH
COAST 500

ROUGH GUIDES

Contents

Introduction to

North Coast 500

The North Coast 500 brings together a route of just over 500 miles (516, to be precise) of stunning coastal scenery in the far north of Scotland. The route may be relatively new – launched by the non-profit North Highland Initiative in 2015 as "Scotland's Route 66" – but the raw and magnificent landscape it traverses has been shaped over thousands of years by geological forces, glaciers and the weather systems of the North Atlantic. It's not always an easy ride; the roads can be thin and winding, and the clouds will descend faster than you thought possible. Yet, experience a glorious sunset that turns a sea loch gold or stumble across yet another empty white-powder beach, and you'll discover the romance of the place, too. Whether you explore opulent castles, sample a dram (or two) of whisky or take to the water on a wildlife safari, the North Coast 500 offers a truly unique touring experience, quite unlike anywhere else in the world.

The route

The North Coast 500 begins in Inverness, the capital of the Highlands, before heading north into the pastoral **Black Isle**, littered with prehistoric sites and home to the pretty resort town of Cromarty. After passing through Tain and crossing the **Dornoch Firth**, you're on the road to John O'Groats. You'll pass through somnolent villages and the impressive **Dunrobin Castle** before arriving at Helmsdale. Beyond, the landscape becomes wilder on the approach to the former fishing town of Wick. After the obligatory photograph at the **John O'Groats** sign and a stop-off at **Dunnet Head** – the northernmost point of Britain – the north coast road passes through rolling grasslands to the surfing town of **Thurso**, a relative metropolis in these parts. Continuing west, past white-sand beaches and crofting townships, you reach the Kyle of Tongue; from this point forward, the landscape becomes more muscular and the weather systems more cinematic.

THE APPLECROSS PASS

FIVE TOP TIPS BEFORE SETTING OFF

- **Do your research** Sit down with a map and plan your route before you go, using www.northcoast500.com and this ebook as inspiration on how to make the most of your trip.
- **Become a North Coast 500 member** The North Coast 500 memberships bring an array of benefits; see www.northcoast500.com/become-a-member.
- **Book ahead** Between Easter and October the North Coast 500 is busy and accommodation books up far in advance. Be sure to plan where to stay months before you leave.
- **Read up on road safety** Roads along the North Coast 500 can be tricky to navigate. Our Basics section (see page 21) includes information on how to stay safe on the roads. See also www.northcoast500.com/top-tips-hitting-route/road-safety.
- **Get kitted out** Pack for all eventualities; you might well have sun in March and hail in August. Check out the North Coast 500's clothing range at www.northcoast500.com/online-shop.

The north coast road continues to **Durness**, launch pad for an epic multi-day hike to **Cape Wrath**, or a less intrepid but nonetheless worthwhile detour into **Smoo Cave**. Heading south, it's a wiggly single-track road towards Assynt, a region that captures the stark, elemental beauty of the Highlands like nowhere else. Through the sleepy settlements of Scourie and Kylesku you reach **Lochinver**, a foodie haven and excellent base for hikes to **Stac Pollaidh** and **Suilven**, just two of many idiosyncratic peaks in the area.

After dancing a ceilidh and stocking up on supplies in the wee fishing town of **Ullapool**, head into Wester Ross, where the road hugs the coast and there are views of Skye and the Western Isles. Whitewashed crofting houses pepper the road to **Gairloch**, where boat trips offer the chance to glimpse dolphins and basking sharks, as well as whales during summer. After passing through the awe-inspiring **Glen Torridon** and a making hair-raising ascent over the **Applecross Pass**, the retreat to Inverness begins.

Of course, this only skims over the significant settlements and sights along the route. It's everything that falls in between – the isolated white-sand beaches, the moody Highland cattle, encounters with friendly locals – that make the North Coast 500 what it is.

Meet the locals

Jon Palmer, The Cheese House
Old Police Station House, Cromarty IV11 8UY •
www.cromartycheese.com

Tell us about yourself I met my wife Emmy in the Netherlands in 2010, at a point when we were both looking to embark on an adventure. Emmy suggested selling cheese, and a year later we set up the only Dutch cheese shop in the UK.

What does the North Coast 500 mean to you? It has been brilliant meeting all the visitors doing the North Coast 500 and curious to taste a slice of the Netherlands in the heart of the Scottish Highlands.

What inspires you the most about your area? Though a diversion from the main North Coast 500 route, Cromarty is an idyllic destination with quirky shops and eating places secreted between old fishermen's cottages and grand merchant houses.

Murray Lamont, Mackays Hotel
Union St, Wick KW1 5ED • www.mackayshotel.co.uk

Tell us about yourself I grew up in the hospitality business and, apart from my student years, have lived in Wick since birth; Mackays has been in my family for nearly 70 years. In the mid-90s we opened Bin Ends, a store supplying good value quality wines, whiskies and spirits.

What does the North Coast 500 mean to you? The North Coast 500 has been declared as one of the best routes in the world – and it's on our doorstep. What you see is what you get: huge empty beaches, seas with an attitude, stacks, hill moors, wildlife and natural history at its best; unspoilt and available.

What inspires you the most about your area? The people in our area are friendly and down to earth, plus the fresh air and pace of life combined with the natural beauty and opportunities make it a wonderful place to be. Wick still has a strong community aspect and that's down to the people who live here.

Dougie Robertson, Highland Ferries

Cromarty IV11 8YN • www.facebook.com/CamusnagaulFerry

Tell us about yourself I've run Highland Ferries for the past five years. We originally operated on the west coast of Scotland before expanding to Cromarty in the summer of 2016.

What does the North Coast 500 mean to you? The North Coast 500 is extremely important to myself and the business. Our ferries are well used by all sorts of people, including cyclists, travellers with motorbikes and motor homes... and even horses.

What inspires you the most about your area? The wildlife on the Cromarty Firth is truly amazing. We have daily sightings of dolphins, which always put a smile on the passengers' faces.

Jo Wyke, Melvich Hotel

Melvich, Thurso KW14 7YJ • www.melvichhotel.co.uk

Tell us about yourself I have lived in Melvich for over ten years, and am now balancing my own Fawlty Towers hotel with an enterprising child and an enthusiastic golden retriever.

What does the North Coast 500 mean to you? The North Coast 500 has essentially opened the gate to the north Highlands and brought plenty more friendly faces to look out over our golden beach here in Melvich. We've enjoyed having it to ourselves for a while now, but it's always better to share the view.

What inspires you the most about your area? The beach. Surfing, running, shell- and driftwood-collecting, dog-walking and Frisbee-throwing, toddler-exploring, bear-hunting, castle-building, problem-solving, calorie-burning, fish-catching and sand-encrusted sandwich-eating. And that's just one afternoon in July.

10

things not to miss

It's difficult to cover many miles along the North Coast 500 without feeling the urge to pull over. What follows is a selective taste of the highlights along the route: natural wonders, hidden beaches and thrilling outdoor activities.

1

1 VISIT THE EDGE OF THE WORLD AT DUNNET HEAD
See page 54

Get a faceful of sea air at the true tip of mainland Britain, with nothing but empty seascapes all the way to Orkney.

2 EXPLORE SMOO CAVE
See page 62

Descend steep steps to the mouth of this cave, and then hop into a rubber dinghy to explore the gloomy caverns that lie within.

3 GETTING LOST IN THE LANES AT CROMARTY
See page 38

A mix-and-match of handsome Georgian townhouses and cute cottages all packaged up in a friendly coastal town.

4 WALKING IN ASSYNT
See page 66

Golden eagles, more deer than cows and strange mountains with poetic names like Suilven – nowhere in the Highlands offers more exhilarating walking opportunities.

5 FRESH LOCAL PRODUCE AND SEAFOOD
See page 26

Hand dived scallops, venison and langoustines are among the best that you'll taste – anywhere.

6 CASTLES
See pages 45 and 67
From the extravagant French-style Dunrobin Castle to the crumbling ruins of Ardveck Castle, exploring these piles is a definitive highlight of the route.

7 SEE THE NORTHERN LIGHTS ON THE NORTH COAST
See page 21
On a cold winter's night with the sky clear of clouds, you may well witness the aurora borealis – or "Mirrie Dancers" – dancing on the horizon. The north coast offers your best chance of a sighting.

8 SOLITUDE AT SANDWOOD BAY
See page 63
It's a two-hour walk – or the start of a two-day hike around Cape Wrath – to this glorious beach at the tip of Britain.

9 WILDLIFE WATCHING ON THE WATER
See page 77
Board a sea cruise from Gairloch for a decent chance of glimpsing porpoises, dolphins and basking sharks. In the height of summer, you may even see a whale.

10 VISIT A DISTILLERY
See page 54
There are a number of world-class whisky distilleries along the route, and gin drinkers can get their fix at Dunnet Bay Distillers.

Itineraries

The beauty of the North Coast 500 is that, despite being one enormous loop, there are countless ways of plotting your itinerary. In the Seven-Day Tour we lay out a classic route, splitting each day into manageable distances and taking in some of the major highlights. The other three itineraries have been tailored for those with a specific interest, whether it be in history, outdoor activities or luxury travel. For more itineraries, see www.northcoast500.com/itinerary.

THE SEVEN-DAY TOUR

This classic (if bite-sized) seven-day tour takes in the very best of the North Coast 500 in a manageable week. Be sure to indulge in the countless diversions that we haven't mentioned below.

❶ Day one: Inverness to Golspie After popping into Glen Ord for a distillery tour and traversing the rolling landscape of the Black Isle, you're on the road north to John O'Groats. *The Storehouse of Foulis* (see page 39) is a great stop-off for lunch, while Dunrobin Castle is a must-see for a taster of the opulent lifestyle of the first Duke of Sutherland. See page 45

❷ Day two: Golspie to John O'Groats Today, you twist and turn through the Caithness landscape. For a crash course in the history of the region, pop into the Timespan Heritage Centre (see page 46). Heading north, via the old herring-fishing town of Wick, you're on the home straight to the folkloric northeasterly point of Great Britain. See page 45

❸ Day three: John O'Groats to Durness Start the day with an obligatory photograph at the famous sign and a coffee from *Stacks Deli, Bakery & Coffee House*. Stop-offs at the Castle of Mey and Dunnet Bay Distillers may slow you down, before taking lunch in surfer hotspot Thurso and heading west to Durness, where the delightful Smoo Cave beckons. See page 51

❹ Day four: Durness to Scourie Early risers should make the four-mile hike to Sandwood Bay before heading south into the heart of Assynt. Here, the landscape becomes otherworldly, with its sugarloaf peaks. Hop on a boat to Handa Island Wildlife Reserve where around 100,000 seabirds come to breed in the summer months. See page 60

Create your own itinerary with Rough Guides. Whether you're after adventure or a family-friendly holiday, we have a trip for you, with all the activities you enjoy doing and the sights you want to see. All our trips are devised by local experts who get the most out of the destination. Visit **www.roughguides.com/trips** to chat with one of our travel agents.

FISHING BOATS IN THE HARBOUR AT JOHN O'GROATS

⊙ Day five: Scourie to Ullapool The white sandy beaches you'll see today could fool you into thinking you're in the Bahamas (if it wasn't for the weather). Take lunch in Lochinver before hooking up with McKenzie Mountaineering for a day in the hills. In the evening, reflect on your day in one of Ullapool's many atmospheric pubs. See page 63

⊙ Day six: Ullapool to Torridon Blow off the cobwebs by getting onto the water. Ewe Canoe offers the chance to paddle and see the coast from a different angle, while the sea tours in Gairloch promise wildlife sightings aboard their glass-bottomed boat. Afterwards, head to the hiker hangout of *Kinlochewe Hotel*. See page 69

⊙ Day seven: Torridon to Inverness It's your final day on the North Coast 500, but there's still a lot to pack in. The Applecross Peninsula promises a remote pub, a smokehouse and a hair-rising road climb. Diversions to the Attadale Gardens and Rogie Falls, and an obligatory mooch around Strathpeffer, should keep morale high on the road back to Inverness where your adventure comes to an end. See page 78

TIME-TRAVELLING THE NORTH COAST 500

From prehistoric sites to Clearance settlements, via foreboding castles and futuristic heritage centres, the North Coast 500 is a road trip through time. In this itinerary, we cover some of the route's most impressive historic and archeological sights, and some lesser-known spots.

❶ Inverness Museum and Art Gallery Before you set off, clue up on the history of the Highlands at this museum, which covers everything from geological formation through to modern times. See page 34

❷ Fortrose Cathedral The unassuming village of Fortrose features one of the Black Isle's most imposing architectural sights; you can explore the crumbling ruins, set on the village green. See page 38

❸ The Pictish Trail Pay a visit to the excellent Groam House Museum to see the famous Rosemarkie Cross Slab, then head north to discover more at the heritage centres in Tain and Portmahomack. See pages 38, 41 and 43

❹ Dunrobin Castle Marvel at the largest house in the Highlands and examine the opulent

furniture, paintings and tapestries that lie within. Time your trip to coincide with the brilliant falconry display. See page 45

❺ Timespan Heritage Centre This hi-tech museum contains insightful interactive displays covering the area's rich history, from the Viking raids to the Clearances. See page 46

❻ Wick The Tardis-like heritage centre in Wick has exhibits on the town's rich history and fascinating artefacts that evoke the heyday of fishing. See page 45

❼ Castle Sinclair Girnigoe This ruined castle emerges from the sea like the sedimentary stacks that surround it. Listen out for the seabirds, whose squawks echo in the old Great Chamber. See page 49

❽ Castle of Mey This sixteenth-century castle was the holiday home of the Queen Mother; look out for the watercolours by Prince Charles, who still visits every July. See page 53

❾ Strathnaver Trail This 24-mile trail spans sites from the Neolithic, Bronze and Iron Age periods, through to crofting settlements cleared during the nineteenth century. Visit the volunteer-run museum beforehand to watch the film and pick up a printout. See page 56

❿ Hippie Balnakeil Discover the unlikely history of Balnakeil, which transformed from a wartime warning station into a hippie commune; the spirit lives on today in the bohemian craft village. See page 62

⓫ Inchnadamph Bone Caves Some amazing discoveries – including human skeletons, an iron blade, and a pin made from walrus ivory – have been made in these limestone caves. See page 64

⓬ Ullapool Museum Run by the local community, this museum contains a number of exhibits detailing the fishing village's past. See page 69

A LUXURY TOUR OF THE NORTH COAST 500

Not everybody relishes the idea of wild camping in a wind-lashed glen, or chowing down on baked beans in a bothy. Fortunately, there are plenty of luxury options for those who prefer the finer things in life. Whether you want to dine at exquisite restaurants or live like a laird in a five-star pile, this itinerary is a good place to start.

❶ Lunch at the Rocpool Reserve Restaurant Don't even think about starting the North Coast 500 on an empty stomach. The *Rocpool Reserve Restaurant* in Inverness is an indulgent lunch spot, serving up Scottish ingredients with a French twist. See page 35

❷ Enjoy a wee dram Some of the region's finest whisky distilleries are based in and around Inverness. Take a private tour and sample a single malt (or a craft beer) at the Uilebheist or Glen Ord distillery. See pages 33, 34 and 36

❸ Explore the Castle of Mey Rub shoulders with the royal family at the Queen Mother's former pad. The well-manicured gardens are perfect for an amble on a sunny day. See page 53

❹ Cocoa Mountain This is probably the most remote chocolate producer in Europe and proud home of the ultra-indulgent "Best Hot Chocolate". See page 62

❺ Sleep in a luxury cabin The brainchild of the people who own Mackay's in Durness, *Croft 103* is a carbon-negative self-catering cabin offering eco-chic with some of the most impressive views along the north coast. See page 62

❻ Linger in foodie Lochinver Lochinver is fast becoming the foodie capital of the Highlands. Take your pick from the *Inver Lodge* restaurant, the *Lochinver Larder* and *Peet's Restaurant*. See page 68

❼ Explore Inverewe Gardens These subtropical-style gardens offer serious escapism in the heart of Wester Ross. Look out for plants from around the world – from Chile to the Himalayas. See page 74

❽ A night at Pool House With views across Loch Ewe, the dining room of the *Pool House* offers the chance to spot seals and otters. Family antiques and rich fabrics make this one of the most elegant small hotels in the Highlands. See page 74

❾ Fine dining at the Torridon Hotel Wrap up your luxury tour of the North Coast 500 with a three-, four- or seven-course menu in this grand old hunting lodge's award-winning restaurant. See page 80

ADVENTURE TOUR OF THE NORTH COAST 500

In many ways, the North Coast 500 is a road trip through one gigantic playground. Bag a Munro

A CANOEIST ON LOCH MAREE, WESTER ROSS

or two, hurtle down a mountain on two wheels and witness whales and dolphins in the wild.

❶ Mountain biking in Golspie Start your adventure tour of the North Coast 500 with some high-octane mountain biking with Highland Wildcat Trails. Black-, red- and blue-graded trails offer options for all abilities. See page 45

❷ Descend the Whaligoe Steps This 365-step stairway descends a steep cliff face, with unprotected vertical drops into the sea. Take care, especially when it's wet and foggy. See page 48

❸ Get blown away at Dunnet Head Feel the forces of nature at mainland Britain's most northerly point. See page 53

❹ Surf's up in Thurso This modest town on the north coast has a reputation among surfers. The waves here are some of the biggest and best in Europe. Bring your wetsuit. See page 54

❺ Explore Smoo Cave Tucked out of sight, at the end of a sea cove, Smoo Cave has impressive rock formations. Weather permitting, you can hop in a dinghy and witness the thundering waterfall that lies within. See page 62

❻ Bag a Munro in Assynt The region's otherworldly terrain offers unforgettable hikes. Take a tour with Hamlet Mountaineering, whose expert guides can lead you to the top of Suilven or Stac Pollaidh. Feeling brave? Give scrambling or climbing a go. See page 66

❼ Wild camping Read up on the rules and regulations before you set out for a wild-camping adventure in Scotland's most stunning scenery and fall asleep under the Highlands' velvet-black sky. See page 25

❽ Marine wildlife safari Take the waters with Hebridean Whale Cruises and keep your eyes peeled for whales (in season), dolphins, porpoises and seals. They also run high-speed RIB tours. See page 77

❾ Gorge scrambling at Loch Torridon Get kitted out by Torridon Outdoors and give gorge scrambling or coasteering a try. For something more sedate, opt for a guided walk or a clay-pigeon shooting experience. See page 78

❿ Sea-kayaking in Wester Ross Discover deserted islands, natural rock arches and white-sand beaches on a sea-kayaking expedition, or head out for a paddle in Loch Maree. See page 77

Moments in history

It's hard to travel around the Scottish Highlands and not have a sense of the stories from history swirling around, from the Stone Age settlers to the empty villages and lonely glens depopulated during the Clearances. What follows is a very brief introduction to a few key periods of Highlands history that you are likely to encounter while travelling along the North Coast 500.

Prehistoric Scotland

Scotland's first inhabitants were **Mesolithic hunter-gatherers**, who arrived in the area south of Oban as the last Ice Age retreated around 8000 BC. There is evidence of their moving onto the islands of Arran, Jura, Rùm, Skye and Lewis, and recent excavation works at a broch in Sand, Applecross, suggest Mesolithic peoples lived in the northwest of Scotland. Around 4500 BC, **Neolithic farmers** from the European mainland began moving into Scotland. To provide enough land for their cereal crops and grazing for their livestock, they cleared large areas of upland forest, usually by fire, and in the process created the characteristic moorland landscapes of much of modern Scotland.

During the **Bronze Age**, new materials led directly to the development of more effective weapons, and the sword and the shield made their first appearance around 1000 BC. Agricultural needs plus new weaponry added up to a state of endemic warfare as villagers raided their neighbours to steal livestock and grain. The Bronze Age peoples responded to the danger by developing a range of defences, among them the spectacular **hillforts**, great earthwork defences, many of which are thought to have been occupied from around 1000 BC.

The Celts to the Picts

Conflict in Scotland intensified in the first millennium BC as successive waves of **Celtic** settlers, arriving from the south, increased competition for land. Around 400 BC, the Celts brought the technology of **iron** with them. These fractious times witnessed the construction of hundreds of **brochs** or fortified towers. The brochs were dry-stone fortifications (built without mortar or cement) often over 40ft in height; a number of brochs can be seen on the North Coast 500, including at Carn liath (near Golspie), Nybster (near John O'Groats), Dun Dornigail (near Tongue) and Clachtoll (see page 67).

In the years following the departure of the Romans in 410 AD, the population of Scotland was split into four groups of people, or nations, dominant in different parts of the country: the Britons, Scotti, Angles and **Picts**. The Pictish Trail connects the main sites in Easter Ross, such as the carved symbol stones in Rosemarkie (see page 38). The Highland Council offers a PDF guide to the trail (see https://bit.ly/2xmB5hV).

TIMELINE

- **4500 BC** Neolithic people move into Scotland
- **100 BC–100 AD** Fortified Iron Age brochs built across Scotland
- **43 AD** Britain is invaded by the Romans
- **83** British tribes defeated by the Romans at the Battle of Mons Graupius
- **410** The Romans withdraw from Britain
- **563** St Columba founds a monastery on Iona and begins to convert the Picts
- **795** Viking raids on the Scottish coast and islands begin
- **843** Kenneth MacAlpine becomes the first King of the Scots and the Picts
- **1040** Macbeth crowned King of Scotland
- **1286** Death of Alexander III sparks the Wars of Scottish Independence
- **1314** Under Robert the Bruce, the Scots defeat the English at the Battle of Bannockburn
- **1320** The Declaration of Arbroath, asserting Scottish independence, is sent to the Pope
- **1371** Robert II becomes the first of the Stewart (Stuart) kings to rule Scotland
- **1488** The Western Isles come under the rule of the Scottish Crown
- **1513** The Scots are defeated by the English at the Battle of Flodden Field
- **1560** The Scottish Church breaks with the Roman Catholic Church
- **1567** Abdication of Mary, Queen of Scots, and accession of James VI (aged 1)
- **1587** Mary, Queen of Scots, is executed on the orders of Queen Elizabeth I
- **1603** James VI of Scotland becomes James I of England
- **1638** National Covenant proclaimed by Scottish Presbyterians
- **1650** The Scots Royalist army is defeated at the Battle of Dunbar by the English under Oliver Cromwell
- **1689** Unsuccessful Jacobite uprising against William of Orange
- **1692** Glencoe massacre: 38 members of the MacDonald clan murdered by anti-Jacobite Campbells
- **1698** 1200 Scots leave to establish a colony in Panama
- **1707** The Act of Union unites the kingdoms of Scotland and England
- **1715** Jacobite uprising against the accession of Hanoverian King George I
- **1746** Bonnie Prince Charlie's Jacobite army is defeated at the Battle of Culloden
- **1762** Beginning of the Highland Clearances
- **1843** The Great Disruption: a third of the Church of Scotland leave to form the Free Church of Scotland
- **1846** Highland potato famine: 1.7 million Scots emigrate
- **1886** Crofters' Holdings Act grants security of tenure in the Highlands and Islands
- **1914–18** 100,000 Scots lose their lives in World War I
- **1928** The National Party of Scotland is formed
- **1939–45** 34,000 Scottish soldiers lose their lives in World War II; 6000 civilians die in air raids
- **1979** Scottish referendum for devolution fails to gain the required forty percent
- **2011** The Scottish National Party wins a majority in the Scottish Parliament
- **2014** Scotland votes to remain part of the United Kingdom in an independence referendum
- **2016** Scotland votes to remain within the EU, but the UK as a whole votes to leave
- **2020** COVID-19 pandemic breaks out
- **2022** Queen Elizabeth II dies at Balmoral Castle, the Scottish royal residence
- **2023** Nicola Sturgeon, Scotland's longest-serving First Minister, resigns citing personal reasons. She is succeeded by Hamza Yousaf

Bonnie Prince Charlie's rebellion

Prince Charles Edward Stuart – better known as **Bonnie Prince Charlie** or "The Young Pretender" – was born in 1720 in Rome, where his father, "The Old Pretender", claimant to the British throne (as the son of James VII), was living in exile with his

Polish wife. At the age of 25, the prince set out for Scotland with two French ships, disguised as a seminarist from the Scots College in Paris. Charles went on to raise the royal standard at Glenfinnan, thus signalling the beginning of the **Jacobite uprising**.

After a decisive victory over government forces at the Battle of Prestonpans, near Edinburgh, and an advance into England, the Jacobites faced superior forces in Derby and retreated to Scotland. The **Kyle of Tongue** was the location of the naval engagement reputed to have sealed the fate of Bonnie Prince's Charlie's rebellion in 1746. After being forced aground by the English frigate HMS *Sheerness*, the Jacobites attempted to flee to Inverness before being ambushed by the anti-Jacobite MacKay clan. Some 1500 men were defeated and taken prisoner, and historians still debate whether the extra men might have altered the outcome of the **Battle of Culloden** three weeks later (see page 35).

The Highland Clearances

The second half of the eighteenth century saw the Highland **population increase** dramatically after the introduction of the easy-to-grow and nutritious potato. The clan chiefs adopted different policies to deal with the new situation. While some encouraged emigration or alternative forms of employment for their tenantry, like fishing and kelping, some landowners developed **sheep runs** on the Highland pastures, introducing hardy breeds like the black-faced Linton and the Cheviot. But extensive sheep farming proved incompatible with a high peasant population, and many landowners decided to clear their estates of tenants, some of whom were forcibly moved to tiny plots of marginal land, where they were to farm as **crofters**. Between 1807 and 1821, around 15,000 people were thrown off their land.

THE HIGHLAND CLANS

The term "**clan**", as it is commonly used to refer to the quasi-tribal associations found in the Highlands of Scotland, only appears in its modern usage in the sixteenth century. In theory, the clan bound together blood relatives who shared a common ancestor, a concept clearly derived from the ancient Gaelic notion of kinship. But in practice many of the clans were of non-Gaelic origin – such as the Frasers, Sinclairs and Stewarts, all of Anglo-Norman descent – and it was the mythology of a common ancestor, rather than the actuality, that cemented the clans together. Furthermore, clans were often made up of people with a variety of surnames, and there are documented cases of individuals changing their names when they swapped allegiances. At the upper end of Highland society was the clan chief (who might have been a minor figure, like MacDonald of Glencoe, or a great lord, like the Duke of Argyll, head of the Campbells), who provided protection for his followers: they would, in turn, fight for him when called upon to do so. Below the clan chief were the chieftains of the septs, or subunits of the clan, and then came the tacksmen, major tenants of the chief to whom they were frequently related. The tacksmen sublet their land to tenants, who were at the bottom of the social scale. The Highlanders wore a simple belted plaid wrapped around the body – rather than the kilt – and not until the late seventeenth century were certain tartans roughly associated with particular clans. The detailed codification of the tartan was produced by the Victorians, whose romantic vision of Highland life originated with George IV's visit to Scotland in 1822, when he appeared in an elaborate version of Highland dress, complete with flesh-coloured tights.

The crofters fight back

The crofters eked out a precarious existence, but they hung on throughout the nineteenth century, often by taking seasonal employment away from home. In the 1880s, however, a sharp downturn in agricultural prices made it difficult for many crofters to pay their rent. This time, inspired by the example of the Irish Land League, they resisted eviction, forming the **Highland Land League** or **Crofters' Party**, and taking part in direct action protests, in particular land occupations, or **land raids**, as they became known. In 1886, in response to the social unrest, Gladstone's Liberal government passed the **Crofters' Holdings Act**, which conceded three of the crofters' demands: security of tenure, fair rents to be decided independently, and the right to pass on crofts by inheritance. But Gladstone did not attempt to increase the amount of land available for crofting, and shortage of land remained a major problem until the **Land Settlement Act** of 1919 made provision for the creation of new crofts. Nevertheless, the population of the Highlands continued to fall into the twentieth century, with many of the region's young people finding city life more appealing.

The Highlands today

After Britain joined the EEC in 1972, the Highlands and Islands were identified as an area in need of special assistance and, in harness with the **Highlands and Islands Development Board**, significant investment was made in the area's infrastructure, including roads, schools, medical facilities and harbours. European funding was also used to support the increased use and teaching of **Gaelic**, and the encouragement of Gaelic broadcasting, publishing and education. At the same time there was a renaissance of Gaelic culture across Scotland as a whole, from the annual National Mod festival of Gaelic literature to the nationwide success of folk-rock bands such as Runrig and Capercaillie, with the result that the indigenous language and culture of the Highlands and Islands, while still vulnerable, are as healthy now as they have been for a century.

The impact of the 2016 "**Brexit**" referendum, in which 52 percent of UK voters opted to leave the EU, has yet to be fully played out, though the UK officially left the EU at the end of January 2020. In the Highlands and Islands, as in Scotland as a whole, around 60 percent voted to remain in the EU; there are still unanswered questions about how this will affect the outcome of a second referendum on Scottish independence, known as "**Indyref2**". The first referendum on Scottish independence took place in 2014, when 55.3 percent of voters voted against independence. Scotland attempted to launch a second bid for independence in 2022, but this was rejected by the UK Supreme Court.

In 2020, Scotland was swept by the **Covid-19 pandemic** along with the rest of the world. Scotland's leadership was praised for its decisive and clear handling of the pandemic.

The resignation of First Minister and leader of the Scottish National Party, Nicola Sturgeon, in February 2023 raised doubts over the future of Scottish independence. In late March, former justice secretary Hamza Yousaf was elected as her successor.

A PEACEFUL SCENE IN CLASHNESSIE IN THE HIGHLANDS

Basics

When to go

"There's no such thing as bad weather, only inadequate clothing", the poet laureate Ted Hughes is alleged to have said when asked why he liked holidaying in Scotland. For those who don't share Hughes' attitude, the weather is probably the single biggest factor to put you off tackling the North Coast 500. It's not that it's always bad, it's just that it is unpredictable: you could just as easily enjoy a week of fabulous sunshine in early April while the rest of the UK was sodden as suffer a week of low-lying fog and drizzle in high summer.

The summer months of June, July and August are the high season, with local school holidays making July and early August the busiest period. Days are generally warm, but the weather is often variable. Daylight hours are long, however, and, in the far north, darkness hardly falls at all in midsummer. The warmer weather does have its drawbacks, though, in the form of clouds of midges, the tiny biting insects that appear around dusk, dawn and in still conditions.

Commonly, May and September provide weather as good as, if not better than, high summer. You're less likely to encounter crowds, and the mild temperatures combined with the changing colours of nature mean both are great for outdoor activities, particularly hiking.

The months of April and October bracket the tourist season for many parts of rural Scotland. Many attractions, tourist offices and guesthouses open for business at Easter and close after the school half term in October. If places do stay open through the winter, it's normally with reduced opening hours; the October-to-March period is also the best time to pick up special offers for accommodation.

Winter days, from November to March, can be crisp and bright, but are more often cold, overcast and all too short. Nevertheless, Hogmanay and New Year has traditionally been a good time to visit Scotland for partying and warm hospitality. On a clear night in winter, visitors in the far north might see displays of the **aurora borealis**, while a fall of snow in the Highlands will prompt plenty of activity in the ski resorts.

Getting there

There are numerous ways of getting to the starting line of the North Coast 500. For most, the quickest, easiest and cheapest way is by plane. Inverness is the traditional gateway to the Highlands, but you'll get a wider selection of flights to Scotland's three main international airports – Glasgow, Edinburgh and Aberdeen – each of which is within a four-hour drive of Inverness.

From England and Wales

If you're heading out to do the North Coast 500 from **England** or **Wales**, flying to Inverness is the quickest option; flights from London (1hr 30min) start at around £40 return with easyJet, while flights from Birmingham (1hr 30min) start at £160 return with Loganair. There are also multiple British Airways and Loganair flights per day from Manchester (1hr 30min), from £120 return, and a daily easyJet service from Bristol (1hr 20min), starting from £40 return. Flights from Cardiff only fly direct to Edinburgh (1hr 10min) and Glasgow (1hr 15min), from £70 return. However, once you add on the cost of transport to and away from the airport, and flying with luggage (most budget airlines charge for all but the smallest cabin bags, except Loganair where 15kg checked baggage is included as standard), the savings on the same journey overland are often minimal. The small airport at Wick has flights from Aberdeen (35min) and Edinburgh (1hr), which are both well connected to airports in England.

Flying with airlines such as Loganair (www.loganair. co.uk), British Airways (www.britishairways.com) and easyJet (http://easyjet.com) may be quick, but coach and train fares can be pretty competitive.

A BETTER KIND OF TRAVEL

At Rough Guides we are passionately committed to travel. We believe it helps us understand the world we live in and the people we share it with – and of course tourism is vital to many developing economies. But the scale of modern tourism has also damaged some places irreparably, and climate change is accelerated by most forms of transport, especially flying. We encourage all our authors to consider the carbon footprint of the journeys they make in the course of researching our guides.

If you book the London–Glasgow/Edinburgh and Glasgow/Edinburgh–Inverness legs separately, return **train** fares can cost as little as £75 (one way; journey time from 8hr), with the very cheapest tickets going on sale twelve weeks in advance. A more flexible or last-minute fare will cost two or three times that amount. New low-cost, fully electric train operator **Lumo** (www.lumo.co.uk) also offers fares from London to Edinburgh from £29 each way (up to 7 trains daily). Another option is the overnight **Caledonian Sleeper** (www.sleeper.scot) from London Euston (daily; journey time to Inverness around 11hr 30min); again, if you book in advance, single overnight fares cost around £50, with no saving on return fares.

The **coach** can be slower than the train but costs less, with a London or Birmingham to Inverness overnight return starting for as little as £29 return (journey time 11hr 30min–13hr).

From Ireland

Travel from Ireland is quickest by plane, with **airfares** from Belfast to Inverness from €150 return. Loganair (http://loganair.co.uk) is the only airline that operates a direct route. Though P&O no longer runs its Larne to Troon service, there remain good **ferry** links with Northern Ireland via Cairnryan, with up to seven sea crossings daily (2hr; single passenger without car from £28; with car from £114). Stena Line also operates up to six services daily from Belfast to Cairnryan (2hr 15min; single passenger without car from £35; with car from £129).

From the US and Canada

Inverness has connections with the US and Canada with BA (http://britishairways.com) via London Heathrow, KLM (www.klm.com) via Amsterdam and Aer Lingus (www.aerlingus.com) via Dublin. Manchester and Birmingham can also give good deals. If you fly nonstop to Scotland from **North America**, you'll arrive in either Glasgow or Edinburgh. The majority of cheap fares, however, route through Amsterdam, London Heathrow, Manchester, Birmingham, Dublin or Paris. To reach any other Scottish airport, you'll definitely need to go via London (7hr), Glasgow or Edinburgh (6–7hr).

Air Transat (www.airtransat.com) has direct flights to Glasgow from Toronto. Return fares for nonstop flights (including taxes) cost around CAN$975. Air Canada (www.aircanada.com) and Lufthansa (www.lufthansa.com) also operate direct routes between Toronto and Edinburgh; return fares for both start at CAN$750.

From Australia and New Zealand

Flight time from **Australia** and **New Zealand** to Scotland is at least 22 hours. There's a wide variety of routes, with those touching down in Southeast Asia the quickest and cheapest on average. To reach Inverness, you usually have to change planes in either London or Amsterdam.

The cheapest direct scheduled flights to London are usually to be found on one of the Asian airlines, such as Malaysia Airlines (www.malaysiaairlines.com) or Thai Airways (www.thaiairways.com). Average **return fares** (including taxes) from eastern cities to London are Aus$1500–2000. Fares from Perth or Darwin cost around Aus$100 less. Return fares from Auckland to London range between NZ$2000 and NZ$3000 depending on the season, route and carrier.

From South Africa

There are no direct flights from **South Africa** to Scotland, so you must change planes en route. The quickest and cheapest route to take is via London, with flight time around eleven hours, usually overnight. **Return fares** from Cape Town to London start from around ZAR12,000; try British Airways (www.britishairways.com) or Virgin Atlantic (www.virginatlantic.com). You'll save money if you buy the next leg of your journey to Scotland separately, through one of the budget airlines.

From mainland Europe

There is a direct flight from Amsterdam to Inverness (one in winter, two in summer). Otherwise, it's a connection via one of the UK airports. **Ferries** run by DFDS Seaways go overnight from Ijmuiden, near Amsterdam, to Newcastle (daily; 16–17hr), less than an hour's drive south of the Scottish border. Return fares start at around €500, for a passenger with a car and an overnight berth (see www.directferries.co.uk).

Getting around

Whether you sit behind a wheel, listening to Gaelic music on the radio, or face the elements on a bicycle or motorbike, or even on foot, your mode of transport will define your experience of the North Coast 500. However you travel, don't rush the route, and rest assured that by the end of the trip you will be a master of the "passing place".

ROAD ETIQUETTE AND SAFETY

- **Use passing places** These are common on single-track roads. Use them to allow oncoming traffic past, and to let any traffic behind overtake.
- **Watch where you stop** Always use appropriate parking spaces and remember not to stop in passing places.
- **Mind your speed** Only drive to the speed limit when it feels safe, and adjust your speed according to the weather conditions.
- **Share the road – with other vehicles** Give cyclists, motorcyclists and walkers plenty of space when passing, and remember to check your blind spot.
- **Share the road – with animals** You'll sometimes be sharing the road with sheep, deer and grumpy cattle. Don't beep: pass slowly and carefully.

By car

In order to **drive** in Scotland you need a current full driving licence. If you're bringing your own vehicle into the country you should also carry your vehicle registration, ownership and insurance documents at all times. In Scotland, as in the rest of the UK, you **drive on the left**. Speed limits are 20–40mph in built-up areas, 70mph on motorways and dual carriageways (freeways) and 60mph on most other roads. As a rule, assume that in any area with street lighting the limit is 30mph.

The AA (0800 887766, www.theaa.com), RAC (0333 2000 999, www.rac.co.uk) and Green Flag (0800 400600, www.greenflag.com) all operate 24-hour **emergency breakdown** services. You may be entitled to free assistance through a reciprocal arrangement with a motoring organization in your home country. If not, you can make use of these emergency services by joining at the roadside, but you will incur a hefty surcharge. In remote areas, you may have a long wait for assistance.

Be aware that the current drink-driving limit (50 milligrams of alcohol per 100 millilitres of blood), bringing Scotland in line with much of Europe, means that even one pint of beer or glass of wine could leave you on the wrong side of the law.

Renting a car

Car rental in Scotland has shot up in price over the last year or two. Most firms charge anything between £50–150 per day, or around £400–900 a week. For peace of mind it is often best to use major chains like Avis (www.avis.co.uk) who operate out of Inverness Airport. Not many smaller local agencies offer leisure car hire in Inverness. With all rentals it's worth checking the terms and conditions carefully; some rentals only allow you to drive a limited number of miles before paying extra.

Automatics are rare at the lower end of the price scale – if you want one, you should book well ahead.

Fuel in the Highlands has always been more expensive than elsewhere in Scotland, and especially so over the past decade. But the current cost of living crisis in the UK and Europe, coupled with the impact of the war in Ukraine, has seen fuel prices rise further. At the time of writing, petrol (gasoline) can be found for around £1.49 per litre, and diesel can be found 15–20p more per litre, although, with such a volatile situation, prices are likely to continue fluctuating wildly.

By camper van

Considering the high demand for accommodation, **camper vans** are an excellent option for driving the North Coast 500. Rates start at around £500 a week in the high season (try www.bunkcampers.com, who have depots in London, Glasgow and Edinburgh) but you will need to book well ahead for the best price. Few companies will rent to drivers with less than one year's experience and most will only rent to people over 21 or 25 and under 70 or 75 years of age.

Scotland's single-track roads weren't designed for large motorhomes, so take it slow and drive carefully. Only park overnight at designated caravan parks or, if wild camping, keep a low profile and stay within fifteen yards of a public road. As with camping (see page 25), leave no trace; you may be able to dispose waste at official campsites. Check www.outdoor access-scotland.com before you go.

By bicycle

Cycling the North Coast 500 is extremely rewarding, though should only be attempted by people with a decent level of fitness and enthusiasm, as there are plenty of steep climbs to tackle along the route. If you average around fifty to sixty miles per day, it will take around nine or ten days to cycle the entire route. Most cyclists opt to complete the route **clockwise**

(this book covers the route anti-clockwise) to avoid a headwind in the more challenging stages through Wester Ross and Assynt. Check www.northcoast500. com/see-do/adventure-outdoors/cycling-the-nc500 for excellent tips on the best cycling routes in the region.

Note that **bike shops** are few and far between along the North Coast 500, particularly along the west coast, so anyone attempting the cycle should be competent in basic bike repairs. Before departure, make sure your bike is fully serviced, capable of carrying your load, and has suitable tyres with plenty of wear left in them. At the very least you should pack a pump, a puncture repair kit, multi-tool, chain oil and spare inner tubes. If you find yourself in an emergency, OrangeFox offers a 24-hour **mobile repair service,** travelling all over the Highlands (www.orangefoxbikes.co.uk). They charge 60p per mile, plus the cost of repairs and parts.

By motorcycle

The North Coast 500 has become increasingly popular among **motorcyclists**, who will find the long, often empty roads some of the most rewarding in the world. Most of the information about driving the route (see box page 23) applies to motorcyclists, and, as with cycling the route, you must travel with the appropriate equipment, high-vis clothing and tools for self-repair.

On foot

Every year, a small, hardy community attempts to **walk** the North Coast 500. Some of the busier roads are unsuitable for walkers, so be sure to plan your route well before setting off and be aware that – for the most part – you will be sharing the route with vehicles. The website https://worldwalking.org offers a platform to track your walking progress, with information on milestones along the route. The website www.visitscotland.com/see-do/active/walking also has information on walking the Highlands.

Accommodation

In common with the rest of Britain, accommodation along the North Coast 500 can be fairly expensive. Budget travellers are well catered for, however, with numerous hostels, and those with money to spend will relish the more expensive country-house hotels. In the middle ground, the standard of some B&Bs, guesthouses and hotels can be disappointing. That said, there are plenty of welcoming, comfortable, well-run places along the route – you'll find the best ones listed in this book.

Booking accommodation

If you decide not to book online, most **tourist offices** will help you find accommodation and **book a room** directly, for which they normally charge a small fee. If you take advantage of this service, it's worth being clear as to what kind of place you'd prefer, as the tourist office quite often selects something quite randomly across the whole range of their membership. Bear in mind, too, that along the North Coast 500 many places are only open for the **tourist season** (Easter to Oct): you'll always find somewhere to stay outside this period, but the choice will be limited.

Hotels

Hotels come in all shapes and sizes. At the upper end of the market, they can be huge country houses and converted castles offering a very exclusive and opulent experience. Most will have a licensed bar and offer both breakfast and dinner, and often lunch as well. Inns (pubs) are making a comeback, as are their modern equivalent, "restaurants with rooms". These will often have only a handful of rooms, but their emphasis on creating an all-round convivial atmosphere, as well as serving top-quality food, often makes them worth seeking out.

Guesthouses and B&Bs

Guesthouses and B&Bs offer the widest and most diverse range of accommodation. VisitScotland uses the term "guesthouse" for a commercial venture that has four or more rooms, at least some of which are ensuite, reserving "B&B" for a predominantly private family home that has only a few rooms to let. In reality, however, most places offer en-suite facilities, and the different names often reflect the pretensions of the owners and the cost of the rooms more than differences in service: in general, guesthouses cost more than B&Bs. Since many B&Bs have only a few rooms, **advance booking** is recommended, especially in the Islands.

Hostels

There's an ever-increasing number of **hostels** in the Highlands to cater for travellers – youthful or otherwise. Most hostels are clean and comfortable,

ACCOMMODATION PRICE CODES

The price ranges given in this book are for a double room in high season, with breakfast included.

£	under £100
££	£100–150
£££	£150–200
££££	£200+

sometimes offering doubles and even singles as well as dormitory accommodation. Others concentrate more on keeping the price as low as possible, simply providing a roof over your head and a few basic facilities. Whatever type of hostel you stay in, expect to pay £10–22 per night.

SYHA Hostelling Scotland (The Scottish Youth Hostels Association; www.hostellingscotland.org. uk) has a number of youth hostels throughout the highlands. All of them offer a range of shared accommodation and private rooms some of which are en suite, plus self-catering facilities, and comfortable lounge areas. Breakfast is available for an additional fee and many of the youth hostels are licensed and sell a range of Scottish craft beers.

If you're not a **member** of one of the hostelling organizations affiliated to **Hostelling International** (HI), you can pay your £15 joining fee (£6/under-25s) at most hostels. **Advance booking** is recommended, and essential at Easter, Christmas and from May to August. You can book online, in person or by phone.

There are plenty of **bothies**, very simple croft accommodation, dotted around the Highlands. They're often without tap, sink, beds, or electricity, but they're free to use and offer a uniquely Scottish experience; the website https://mountainbothies.org. uk has more information on bothies in the Highlands.

There are also loads of **independent hostels** across the Highlands. These are usually laidback places with no membership, fewer rules, mixed dorms and no curfew. You can find most of them in the annually updated *Independent Hostel Guide* (www.scottish-hostels.com). Many of them are also affiliated to Scottish Independent Hostels (http://hostel-scotland. co.uk), which has a programme of inspection and an excellent hostel search engine complete with booking, available free online.

Camping

There are dozens of **caravan and camping parks** around the Highlands, most of which are open from

April to October. The majority of sites charge about £10–15 for two people with a car to pitch a tent, and are usually well equipped, with shops, a restaurant, a bar and, occasionally, sports facilities. Most of these, however, are aimed principally at caravans, trailers and motorhomes, and generally don't offer the tranquil atmosphere and independence that those travelling with just a tent are seeking.

That said, peaceful and **informal sites** do exist, though they are few and far between. Many **hostels** allow camping, and farmers will usually let folk camp on their land for free or for a nominal sum.

Scotland's relaxed land access laws allow **wild camping** in open country. The basic rule is "leave no trace", but for a guide to good practice, visit www. outdooraccess-scotland.scot.

The majority of **caravans** are permanently moored nose to tail in the vicinity of some of the Highlands' finest scenery; others are positioned singly in back gardens or amid farmland. Some can be booked for self-catering, and with prices starting at around £100 a week, this can work out as one of the cheapest options if you're travelling with kids in tow.

If you're planning to do a lot of camping at official camping and caravanning sites, it might be worthwhile joining the **Camping and Caravanning Club** (www.campingandcaravanningclub.co.uk).

Self-catering

A number of visitors driving the North Coast 500 with a bit more time on their hands opt for **self-catering**, booking a cottage or apartment for a few days or longer and often saving themselves a considerable amount of money by doing so. In some cases, the minimum period of rental is a week, though increasingly, with the rise of websites like www.airbnb.com, owners are becoming more flexible. The least you can expect to pay in the high season is around £350 per week for a place sleeping four, but something special, or somewhere in a popular tourist area, might cost £750 or more.

Food and drink

The remoteness along parts of the North Coast 500 will inevitably restrict your eating and drinking choices. It's often a good idea to plan meal locations ahead as you might find serving times restrictive or popular restaurants booked out, particularly in summer. Stocking up on picnic food from a good local deli is also worthwhile.

Breakfast

In most hotels and B&Bs you'll be offered a **Scottish breakfast**, similar to its English counterpart of sausage, bacon and egg, but typically with the addition of black pudding (blood sausage) and potato scones. Porridge is another likely option, as is fish in the form of kippers, smoked haddock or even kedgeree. Scotland's staple drink, like England's, is **tea**, drunk strong and with milk, though **coffee** is just as readily available everywhere.

Lunches and snacks

The most common lunchtime fare in Scotland remains the **sandwich**. A bowl or cup of hearty **soup** is a typical accompaniment, particularly in winter. A **pub lunch** is often an attractive alternative. Bar menus generally have standard, filling but unambitious options including soup, sandwiches, scampi and chips, or steak pie and chips, with vegetarians suffering from a paucity of choice. That said, some bar food is freshly prepared and filling, equalling the a la carte dishes served in the adjacent hotel restaurant. Note that kitchens often close at 2pm till the evening serving.

Restaurants are often, though not always, open at lunchtimes, when they tend to be less busy and generally offer a shorter menu compared with their evening service. For morning or afternoon snacks, as well as light lunches, **tearooms** are a common feature where you will often find decent home baking.

As for **fast food**, chip shops, or chippies, abound – the best are often found in coastal towns within sight of the fishing boats. Deep-fried battered fish is the standard choice. In remote areas with very few facilities, general stores often sell sausage rolls and scotch pies; most will be happy to heat them up for you.

Evening meals

There's no doubt that, as with the rest of the UK, eating out in the Highlands can be expensive. Wine in restaurants is marked up strongly, so you'll often pay £15 for a bottle selling for £5 in the shops; house wines generally start around the £10 mark.

In more remote parts along the North Coast 500, ask for advice about nearby options for your **evening meal**. Many B&Bs and guesthouses will cook you dinner, but you must book ahead and indicate any dietary requirements. Note that some pub and hotel kitchens stop serving as early as 8pm.

As for **restaurants**, standards vary enormously, but independent restaurants using high-quality local produce are now found all over the region. Less predictable are hotel restaurants, many of which serve non-residents. Some can be very ordinary despite the descriptions on the a la carte menu. You could easily end up paying £40 a head for a meal with wine.

Among traditional **desserts**, "clootie dumpling" is a sweet, stodgy fruit pudding bound in a cloth and cooked for hours, while Cranachan, made with toasted oatmeal steeped in whisky and folded into whipped cream flavoured with fresh raspberries is considered more refined.

Food shopping

Most Scots get their supplies from supermarkets, but you're increasingly likely to come across good delis, farm shops and specialist **food shops**. Many stock local produce alongside imported delicacies, as well as organic fruit and veg, specialist drinks such as locally brewed beer, freshly baked bread, and sandwiches and other snacks for takeaway. It's a good idea to shop local so the money stays local.

Scotland is notorious for its sweet tooth, and **cakes and puddings** are taken very seriously. Bakeries with extensive displays of iced buns, cakes and cream-filled pastries are a typical feature of any Scottish high street, while home-made shortbread, scones or tablet (a hard, crystalline form of fudge) are considered great treats.

Drinking

As in the rest of Britain, Scottish **pubs**, which originated as travellers' hostelries and coaching inns, are the main social focal points of any community. Pubs along the North Coast 500 vary hugely, from old-fashioned inns with open fires and a convivial atmosphere to raucous theme-pubs with jukeboxes and satellite TV.

Scotland's drink-driving laws are very strict, so it's wise to avoid drinking at all if you intend to drive. However, the licensing laws are very relaxed. Pub **opening hours** are generally 11am to 11pm, but some places stay open later. Whatever time the pub closes, "last orders" will be called by the bar staff about fifteen minutes before closing time to allow "drinking-up time". In general, you have to be 16 to enter a pub unaccompanied, though some places are relaxed about children. The legal drinking age is 18.

Whisky

Whisky – *uisge beatha*, or the "water of life" in Gaelic – has been produced in Scotland, primarily in the Highlands and Islands, since the fifteenth century, but only really took off in popularity after the 1780 tax on claret made wine too expensive for most people. The taxman soon caught up with whisky, however, and drove the stills underground. Today, many distilleries operate on the site of simple cottages that once distilled the stuff illegally.

Despite the dominance of the blended whiskies such as Johnnie Walker, Bell's, Teacher's and The Famous Grouse, **single malt whisky** is infinitely superior and, as a result, a great deal more expensive. Single malts vary in character enormously depending on the amount of peat used for drying the barley, the water used for mashing and the type of oak cask used in the maturing process. Malt whisky is best drunk with a splash of water to release its distinctive flavours.

Beer

Traditional Scottish beer is a thick, dark ale known as **heavy**, served at room temperature in pints or half-pints, with a full head. Quite different in taste from English "bitter", heavy is a more robust, sweeter beer with less of an edge. All of the big-name breweries – McEwan's, Tennent's, Bellhaven and Caledonian – produce a reasonable selection of heavies, available at most pubs. However, if you really want to discover Scottish beer, look out for the products of small **local breweries**, many based in the Highlands and Islands. Look out, too, for Froach, available mostly in bottles, a delicious, lighter-coloured ale made from heather according to an ancient recipe.

Water and soft drinks

Scotland produces a prodigious amount of **mineral water**, much of which is exported – tap water is clean and perfectly palatable in most parts of the country, including the areas of the Highlands where it's tinged the colour of weak tea by peat in the ground.

Travel essentials

Costs

The Highlands are a relatively **expensive** place to visit, with travel, food and accommodation costs higher than the EU average. The minimum expenditure for a couple staying in hostels or camping is in the region of £35 each a day. Staying at budget B&Bs, eating at unpretentious restaurants and visiting the odd tourist attraction means spending at least £75 each per day. If you're renting a car, staying in comfortable B&Bs or hotels and eating well, you should reckon on at least £125 a day per person.

Electricity

The current in Scotland is the **EU standard** of approximately 230v AC. All sockets are designed for British three-pin plugs, which are totally different from the rest of the EU.

Emergencies

For **police**, **fire** and **ambulance** services phone 999

Entry requirements

Citizens of EU, US, Canada, Australia, New Zealand, Israel, Japan, as well as many Caribbean and Latin American countries, can enter Britain with just a **passport**, for up to six months. Citizens of most other countries require a **visa**, obtainable from the British consulate or mission office in the country of application.

NATIONAL TRUST FOR SCOTLAND

Many of Scotland's most treasured sights – from castles and country houses to islands, gardens and tracts of protected landscape – come under the control of the privately run **National Trust for Scotland** (www.nts.org.uk); we've quoted "NTS" for each site reviewed in this Guide. The NTS has an admission fee for most places, and these can be quite high, especially for the more grandiose estates.

It's worth considering an **annual membership**, or one of the time-limited passes, if you're thinking of visiting a number of NTS sights.

ROUGH GUIDES TRAVEL INSURANCE

Rough Guides has teamed up with WorldNomads.com to offer great travel insurance deals. Policies are available to residents of over 150 countries, with cover for a wide range of adventure sports, 24hr emergency assistance, high levels of medical and evacuation cover and a stream of travel safety information. Roughguides.com users can take advantage of their policies online 24/7, from anywhere in the world – even if you're already travelling. And since plans often change when you're on the road, you can extend your policy and even claim online. Roughguides.com users who buy travel insurance with WorldNomads.com can also leave a positive footprint and donate to a community development project. For more information go to www.roughguides.com/travel-insurance.

Note that visa regulations are subject to frequent changes. If you visit www.ukvisas.gov.uk, you can download the full range of **application forms** and information leaflets, and find out the contact details of your nearest embassy or consulate, as well as the rules regarding visa extensions. In addition, an independent charity, the Immigration Advisory Service or IAS (https://iasservices.org.uk/tourist-visit-visas), offers free and confidential advice to anyone applying for entry clearance into the UK.

LGBTQ+

While there's no **LGBTQ+ scene** as such out in the Highlands, many Scots have a positive – or at least neutral – opinion of LGBTQ+ people, reflected in positive media coverage by the likes of the *Herald on Sunday*. In more remote areas, and in particular in those areas where religious observance is high, attitudes tend to be more conservative, and gay and lesbian locals are extremely discreet about their sexuality.

Health

This book was produced shortly after a period of continuing uncertainty caused by the Covid-19 pandemic; visitors to Scotland should check national guidance at www.gov.uk/guidance/covid-19-coronavirus-restrictions-what-you-can-and-cannot-do for current requirements (such as mask-wearing).

Pharmacists (known as chemists in Scotland) can dispense only a limited range of drugs without a doctor's prescription. Most pharmacies are open standard shop hours, though there are also late-night branches in large cities and at 24-hour supermarkets.

If your condition is serious enough, you can turn up at the Accident and Emergency (A&E) department of a local **hospital** for complaints that require immediate attention. Obviously, if it's an absolute emergency, you should ring for an ambulance (999).

Air ambulances also operate in remote areas. These services are free to all.

Insurance

It's a good idea to take out **travel insurance** before travelling to cover against theft, loss and illness or injury. For non-UK citizens, it's worth checking whether you are already covered before you buy a new policy. If you need to take out insurance, you might want to consider the travel insurance deal we offer: see www.roughguides.com for details.

Internet

Internet cafés are still found occasionally in the Highlands, but wi-fi is now the best way to get online, with free networks available at most B&Bs and hostels, although connections can still be poor in remote areas. Network coverage for 3G, 4G and 5G is patchy in the Highlands.

Maps

The most comprehensive maps of Scotland are produced by the **Ordnance Survey** or OS (www.ordnancesurvey.co.uk), renowned for their accuracy and clarity. If you're planning on stopping for a walk of more than a couple of hours' duration, it is strongly recommended that you carry the relevant OS map and familiarize yourself with how to navigate using it. All OS maps now also come with a smartphone download.

In any walking district of Scotland you'll find the relevant maps in local shops or tourist offices.

Virtually every service station in Scotland stocks at least one large-format **road atlas**. For getting between major towns and cities a sat nav or GPS-enabled smartphone is hard to beat, but you'll have less luck in rural areas, where landmarks and even entire roads can be positioned incorrectly.

Money

The basic unit of **currency** in the UK is the pound sterling (£), divided into 100 pence (p). Coins come in denominations of 1p, 2p, 5p, 10p, 20p, 50p, £1 and £2. Bank of England £5, £10, £20 and £50 banknotes are legal tender in Scotland; in addition, the **Bank of Scotland** (HBOS), the **Royal Bank of Scotland** (RBS) and the **Clydesdale Bank** issue their own banknotes in all the same denominations, plus a £100 note. For the most up-to-date exchange rates, check the useful website www.xe.com.

Credit/debit cards are by far the most convenient way to carry your money, and most hotels, shops and restaurants in Scotland accept the major brand cards. In every sizeable town in Scotland, and in some surprisingly small places too, you'll find a branch of at least one of the big Scottish high-street **banks**, usually with an **ATM** attached. General **banking hours** are Monday to Friday from 9 or 9.30am to 4 or 5pm, though some branches are open until slightly later on Thursdays. Post offices charge **no commission**, have longer opening hours, and are therefore often a good place to change money and cheques. In towns with no banks, mobile branch vans are sometimes available. Lost or stolen credit/debit cards should be reported to the police and the following numbers: MasterCard 0800 964767; Visa 0800 891725.

CALLING HOME FROM ABROAD

To make an international call, dial the international access code (in Scotland it's 00), then the destination's country code, before the rest of the number. Note that the initial zero is omitted from the area code when dialling Ireland, Australia and New Zealand from abroad.

Australia international access code + 61

Ireland international access code + 353

New Zealand international access code + 64

South Africa international access code + 27

US and Canada international access code + 1

Opening hours and public holidays

Traditional **shop hours** in Scotland are Monday to Saturday 9am to 5.30 or 6pm. In the bigger towns, many places now stay open on Sundays and late at night on Thursdays or Fridays. Large supermarkets typically stay open till 8pm or 10pm and a few manage 24-hour opening (excluding Sunday). However, there are also plenty of towns and villages where you'll find very little open on a Sunday. Many small towns along the North Coast 500 also retain an "**early closing day**" often Wednesday – when shops close at 1pm, and you'll find precious few attractions open outside the tourist season (Easter to Oct), though ruins, parks and gardens are normally accessible year-round. Note that last entrance can be an hour (or more) before the published closing time.

PUBLIC HOLIDAYS

Official **bank holidays** in Scotland operate on: January 1 and 2; Good Friday; the first and last Monday in May; the last Monday in August; St Andrew's Day (Nov 30); Christmas Day (Dec 25); and Boxing Day (Dec 26). In addition, all Scottish towns have one-day holidays in spring, summer and autumn – dates vary from place to place but normally fall on a Monday. While many local shops and businesses close on these days, few tourist-related businesses observe the holidays, particularly in the summer months.

Phones

Public **payphones** are still occasionally found in the Highlands, though with the ubiquity of mobile phones, they're seldom used.

If you're taking your **mobile phone** with you to Scotland, check with your service provider whether your phone will work abroad and what the call charges will be. Calls to destinations further afield, however, are still unregulated and can be prohibitively expensive. Unless you have a tri-band phone, it's unlikely that a mobile bought for use in the US will work outside the States and vice versa. Mobiles in Australia and New Zealand generally use the same system as the UK so should work fine. All the main UK networks cover the Highlands, though you'll still find many places in among the hills or out on the islands where there's **no signal** at all. If you're in a rural area and having trouble with reception, simply ask a local where the strongest signals are found nearby.

Time

Greenwich Mean Time (GMT) – equivalent to Co-ordinated Universal Time (UTC) – is used from the end of October to the end of March; for the rest of the year the country switches to **British Summer Time** (BST), one hour ahead of GMT.

Tipping

There are no fixed rules for **tipping**. If you think you've received good service, particularly in restaurants or cafés, you may want to leave a tip of ten percent of the total bill (unless service has already been included). It's not normal, however, to leave tips in pubs. The only other occasions when you'll be expected to tip are in hairdressers, taxis and smart hotels, where porters, bellboys and table waiters rely on being tipped to bump up their often dismal wages.

Tourist information

The official tourist board is known as **VisitScotland** (www.visitscotland.com) and runs **tourist offices** (officially called iCentres, but also known as Visitor Information Centres) in 26 Scottish cities and towns. Opening hours are often fiendishly complex and can change at short notice, but they are usually open year-round.

As well as being stacked full of souvenirs and other gifts, most iCentres have a decent selection of leaflets, displays, maps and books relating to the local area. The staff are usually helpful and will do their best to help with enquiries about accommodation, local transport, attractions and restaurants, although it's worth being aware that they're sometimes reluctant to divulge information about local attractions or accommodation options that are not paid-up members of the Tourist Board, and a number of perfectly decent guesthouses and the like choose not to pay the fees.

Travellers with disabilities

Scottish attitudes towards travellers with **disabilities** still lag behind advances towards independence made in North America and Australia. Access to many public buildings has improved, with legislation ensuring that all new buildings have appropriate facilities. Some hotels and a handful of B&Bs have one or two adapted rooms, usually on the ground floor and with step-free showers, grab rails and wider doorways. It's worth keeping in mind, however, that installing ramps, lifts, wide doorways and disabled toilets is impossible in many of Scotland's older and historic buildings.

Car rental firm Avis will fit their cars (generally automatics only) with hand controls for free as long as you give them a few days' notice.

For more information and advice, contact Capability Scotland (0131 337 9876, www.capability.scot).

Inverness to the Black Isle and beyond

Make the most of the international cuisine and high street conveniences in Inverness, for this will be your last taste of cosmopolitan living for some time. The only city in the Highlands is over a hundred miles from any other major settlement, and its population – just shy of fifty thousand – exceeds that of Caithness and Sutherland combined. It's a quick escape west out of the city centre, beyond which the lowland pastoral landscape of the Black Isle beckons. Soon after leaving Inverness you'll catch a glimpse of the hills to the west; a taster for the exhilarating journey that lies ahead.

1

HIGHLIGHTS

❶ **Whisky distillery tours** Visit Uilebheist, the first whisky distillery in Inverness for 40 years, and take tours of Glen Ord, one of the oldest and largest distilleries in the Highlands. See page 33 and 36

❷ **The Pictish trail** Look out for the brown road signs and hunt down Pictish sites in the Black Isle. Rosemarkie's Groam House Museum brings the era to life with its fifteen well-preserved standing stones. See page 38

❸ **Dolphin spotting** Overlooking the Moray Firth, Chanonry Point is one of the best places

in Britain to see bottlenose dolphins. Bring binoculars and bide your time. See page 36

❹ **Getting lost in Cromarty** This higgledy-piggledy port town is ideal for a leisurely amble; the Georgian townhouses here are among the finest in the Highlands. See page 38

❺ **Fly-fishing** Whether you've caught a catalogue of fish in your time or never cast a line before, the team at Trout Quest offer exceptional trout and salmon fly-fishing trips. See page 39

While this first stage of the North Coast 500 may not be the most dramatic in terms of scenery, tourers should resist the temptation to rush through. **Inverness** warrants a day or two of exploration and the **Black Isle** has a trail of fascinating Pictish sites signposted off the A9, and the towns of **Strathpeffer** and **Cromarty** represent two of the most elegant settlements in the Highlands. For those wanting a taste of the great outdoors, **Rogie Falls** offer the chance to witness salmon leaping in the height of summer and the dolphin-spotting opportunities here are the finest in the whole of Scotland.

GETTING AROUND INVERNESS TO THE BLACK ISLE AND BEYOND

The roads around Inverness are by far the busiest that you'll encounter on the North Coast 500, but the escape from the city is painless. Whether you arrive at the airport, the train station or the bus station, it's a short journey to the A862: a pleasant alternative to the busier but more direct A9. **Drivers**, **motorcyclists** and **larger vehicles** on this first leg of the North Coast 500 will enjoy flat, mainly 60mph roads, none being single-track. **Cyclists** face a gentle uphill pedal immediately out of Inverness, though the elevation in these parts is modest compared to the north and west coast. For most of the route from Inverness to the Dornoch Firth Bridge, cyclists should aim to take the quieter B roads and avoid the A9. Adventurous **walkers** can also begin the 147-mile coastal John o'Groats Trail from Inverness.

Inverness and around

Straddling a nexus of major road and rail routes, **INVERNESS** is the busy hub of the Highlands and the starting point of the North Coast 500. Crowned by a pink crenellated **castle** and lavishly decorated with flowers, the city centre still has some hints of its medieval street layout, though unsightly concrete blocks do an efficient job of masking it. Within walking distance of the centre are peaceful spots along by the Ness, leafy parks and friendly B&Bs located in prosperous-looking stone houses.

The sheltered **harbour** and proximity to the open sea made Inverness an important entrepôt and shipbuilding centre during medieval times. David I, who first imposed a feudal system on Scotland, erected a castle on the banks of the Ness to oversee maritime trade in the early twelfth century, promoting it to royal burgh status soon after. Bolstered by receipts from the lucrative export of leather, salmon and timber, the town grew to become the kingdom's most prosperous northern outpost, and an obvious target for the marauding Highlanders who plagued this remote border area. A second wave of growth occurred during the eighteenth century as the Highland cattle trade flourished. The arrival of the **Caledonian Canal** and **rail** links with the east and south brought further prosperity, heralding a tourist boom that reached a fashionable zenith in the Victorian era, fostered by the royal family's enthusiasm for all things Scottish.

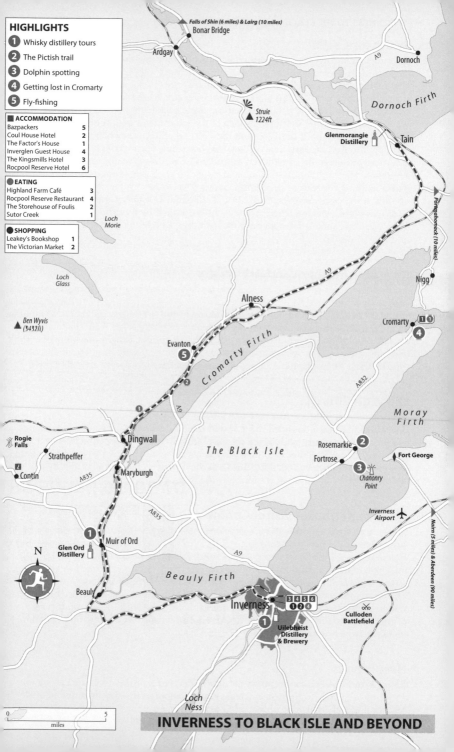

HIGHLIGHTS

1. Whisky distillery tours
2. The Pictish trail
3. Dolphin spotting
4. Getting lost in Cromarty
5. Fly-fishing

■ ACCOMMODATION

Bazpackers	5
Coul House Hotel	2
The Factor's House	1
Inverglen Guest House	4
The Kingsmills Hotel	3
Rocpool Reserve Hotel	6

● EATING

Highland Farm Café	3
Rocpool Reserve Restaurant	4
The Storehouse of Foulis	2
Sutor Creek	1

● SHOPPING

Leakey's Bookshop	1
The Victorian Market	2

Falls of Shin (6 miles) & Lairg (10 miles)

Bonar Bridge

Ardgay

Dornoch

Dornoch Firth

Struie
▲ 1224ft

Glenmorangie
Distillery

Tain

Portmahomack (10 miles)

Loch Morie

Nigg

Loch Glass

Alness

Cromarty

Ben Wyvis
(3432ft)

Evanton

Cromarty Firth

A9

Moray Firth

Rogie Falls

Strathpeffer

Dingwall

The Black Isle

Rosemarkie

Fort George

Contin

A835

Maryburgh

Fortrose

Chanonry Point

A832

Inverness Airport

Glen Ord Distillery

Muir of Ord

A835

A9

Beauly

Beauly Firth

Inverness

Culloden Battlefield

Nairn (5 miles) & Aberdeen (90 miles)

Uilebheist Distillery & Brewery

N

Loch Ness

0   miles   5

INVERNESS TO BLACK ISLE AND BEYOND

1

Inverness Castle

Looming above the city and dominating the horizon is **Inverness Castle**, a predominantly nineteenth-century red-sandstone building perched above the river. The original castle formed the core of the ancient town, which had rapidly developed as a port trading with Europe after its conversion to Christianity by St Columba in the sixth century. Robert the Bruce wrested the castle back from the English during the Wars of Independence, destroying much of the structure in the process, and while the Jacobites held it in both the 1715 and the 1745 rebellions, they blew it up to prevent it falling into government hands. Today's edifice is not open to the general public but is currently undergoing a major refurbishment to become a visitor centre and tourist attraction. There are various plaques and statues in the castle grounds, including a small plinth marking the start of the 73-mile Great Glen Way.

South of the castle, on Ness Bank, lies the **Uilebheist Distillery and Brewery** (www. uilebheist.com), which opened in 2022 and is powered by water from the River Ness. There are tours and experiences on offer, including a blending masterclass and paired tasting sessions (see website for prices).

Inverness Museum and Art Gallery

Castle Wynd • Tues–Sat April–Oct 10am–5pm, Nov–March noon–4pm • Free • www.highlifehighland.com/inverness-museum-and-art-gallery

Below the castle, the revamped **Inverness Museum and Art Gallery** on Castle Wynd offers an insight into the social history of the Highlands, with treasures from the Pictish and Viking eras, taxidermy exhibits such as "Felicity" the puma, caught in Cannich in 1980, and interactive features including an introduction to the Gaelic language. It also houses the Highland Photographic Archive, and has impressive temporary art exhibitions.

Old High Church

Church St, next to Leakey's bookshop • Grounds open to public • Free

The **Old High Church**, founded in 1171 and rebuilt on several occasions since, stands just back from the east bank of the river on Church Street, hemmed in by a walled graveyard. Those Jacobites who survived the massacre of Culloden were brought here and incarcerated prior to their execution in the cemetery. If you look carefully you may see the bullet holes left on gravestones by the firing squads.

Scottish Kiltmaker Visitor Centre

In the Highland House of Fraser shop at 4–9 Huntly St, on the river's west bank • Daily 9am–10pm; kilt-making demonstrations daily 9am–5pm • Charge • www.highlandhouseoffraser.com

Entered through the factory shop, the **Scottish Kiltmaker Visitor Centre** is an imaginative small attraction, which sets out everything you ever wanted to know about tartan, and displays some of the outfits worn in the *Braveheart* and *Rob Roy* films. There's an interesting seven-minute film shown on the hour, and on weekdays you can watch various tartan items being made in the workshop. The finished products are, of course, on sale in the showroom downstairs, along with all manner of Highland knitwear, woven woollies and classy Harris tweed.

Ness Islands

From **St Andrews Episcopal Cathedral**, on the west bank of the river, you can wander a mile or so upriver to the peaceful **Ness Islands**, an attractive, informal public park reached and linked by footbridges. Laid out with mature trees and shrubs, the islands are the favourite haunt of local anglers.

Caledonian Canal

Half a mile upstream from the Ness Islands park, the River Ness runs close to the **Caledonian Canal**, designed by Thomas Telford in the early nineteenth century as a link between the east and west coasts, joining lochs Ness, Oich, Lochy and Linnhe. Today its main use is recreational, and there are cruises through part of it to Loch Ness, while the towpath provides relaxing walks with good views.

Culloden

6 miles east of Inverness off the B9006 • Visitor centre daily: April, May, Sept & Oct 9am–5.30pm; June–Aug 9am–6pm; Nov, Dec, Feb & March 10am–4pm • Charge • NTS • www.nts.org.uk/culloden

The windswept moorland of **CULLODEN** witnessed the last-ever battle on British soil when, on April 16, 1746, the Jacobite cause was finally subdued – a turning point in the history of the Scottish nation. Today, this historic site attracts more than 200,000 visitors annually. Your first stop should be the superb **visitor centre**, where costumed actors and interactive technology are employed to tell the tragedy of Culloden through the words, songs and poetic verse of locals and soldiers who experienced it. The *pièce de résistance* is the powerful "battle immersion theatre" where visitors are surrounded by lifelike cinematography and the sounds of the raging, bloody fight.

ARRIVAL AND INFORMATION INVERNESS AND AROUND

By plane Inverness Airport is 9 miles east of the city centre on the A96.

By train The train station is on Station Square, just off Academy Street, to the northeast of the centre.

By bus The main bus hub is just north of the train station, close to the public library.

Tourist office The tourist office is at 36 High Street, half-way down the pedestrianised street (Mon & Wed–Sat 9am–5pm, Tues 10am–5pm, and Sunday 10am–4pm). It stocks a wide range of literature, including free maps of the city and its environs, and the staff can book day trips and local accommodation for a nominal fee.

GETTING AROUND

Ticket to Ride at The Pavilion Bellfield Park; www. tickettoridehighlands.co.uk. Rents out decent bikes from £40/day.

Avis 01463 709517; www.avis.co.uk. Reliable and friendly service from a major car hire agency, with a range of all-weather vehicles at competitive prices. Pick-up from Inverness Airport and return to the same branch, or at another Avis UK location.

ACTIVITIES INVERNESS

Walk Inverness https://walkinverness.com. Join friendly Invernessian guide Cath for a look around the Gateway to the Highlands, and realise why it's much more than just that. You'll delve into the history and architecture of one of Scotland's most underrated cities, as Cath imparts years of local knowledge: from notable local clans to the city's infamous castle, to supposed Outlander scene locations and where best to go for a pint. You won't miss her – look for the red hat. 2hr walking tours £14; 11am daily.

ACCOMMODATION AND EATING

Bazpackers 4 Culduthel Rd; www.bazpackershostel. co.uk. The most cosy and relaxed of the city's hostels, with more than thirty beds, including three doubles and two twins; some dorms are mixed. Good location in an 1826 townhouse, great views and a garden, which is used for barbecues. **£**

Inverglen Guest House 7 Abertarff Rd; www. inverglenguesthouse.co.uk. Supremely cosy and colourful rooms in a handsome villa. Smoked Scottish salmon is on the breakfast menu, and they run single-day or two-day photography workshops, with trips to nearby glens and castles. **££**

The Kingsmills Hotel Culcabock Rd; www.kingsmills hotel.com. 4-star hotel and spa a short drive from the city centre. Rooms are comfortable, spacious and well-equipped, and use of leisure facilities is inclusive. Highly commended whisky bar and restaurant. **£££**

★ **Rocpool Reserve Hotel and Restaurant** Culduthel Rd; https://rocpool.com. This acclaimed hotel has minimal but luxurious rooms plus a swanky restaurant. This is one of the city's smartest dining options, with contemporary decor, attentive staff and deliciously rich food. The a la carte menu focuses heavily on Scottish produce. Mon–Sat noon–2pm & 7–10pm. **££££**

SHOPPING

Leakey's Bookshop Church St; https://leakeysbookshop.com. A roaring log fire, rare books and vintage maps await at Scotland's largest secondhand bookshop, located in an old Gaelic church. Mon–Sat 10am–5.30pm.

The Victorian Market Academy St; www.thevictorianmarket.com. Nineteenth-century shopping arcade of local wares; newly refurbished food and drink hall adds regularly rotating roster of musicians and food traders. Sun–Tues 8am–6pm, Wed–Sat until 7pm.

The Black Isle and around

The **east coast** of the Highlands is nowhere near as spectacular as the west, and feels more lowland than highland. Heading north from Inverness, you're soon into the **Black Isle** – not an island at all, but a peninsula whose rolling hills, prosperous farms and deciduous woodland make it more reminiscent of Dorset or Sussex than the Highlands.

The Black Isle is littered with **prehistoric sites**, but the main incentive to detour east off the A9 is **Cromarty**, a picturesque fishermen's town that is arguably the highlight of the entire Highlands' east coast. If you're heading this way with your own transport, you can stop off at a string of villages along the south coast for a modest cultural fix, while **Chanonry Point** is among the best **dolphin-spotting** sites in Europe (see box).

Glen Ord Distillery

West Rd, Muir of Ord • Daily 10am–5pm; closed Christmas & New Year • Charge • www.malts.com/en-row/distilleries/the-singleton-of-glen-ord

Opened in 1838 by the MacKenzie family, the **Glen Ord Distillery** is today one of the largest whisky producers in the Highlands, and the only one in the area with its own

---

THE DOLPHINS OF THE MORAY FIRTH

The **Moray Firth**, a great wedge-shaped bay forming the eastern coastline of the Highlands, is one of only three areas of UK waters that support a resident population of **dolphins**. Around 200 of these beautiful, intelligent marine mammals live in the estuary, the most northerly breeding ground in Europe for this particular species – the bottlenose dolphin (*Tursiops truncatus*) – and you stand a good chance of spotting a few, from either the shore or a boat.

One of the best places in Scotland, if not in Europe, to look for them is **Chanonry Point**, on the Black Isle – a spit of sand protruding into a narrow, deep channel, where converging currents bring fish close to the surface, and thus the dolphins close to shore; a rising tide is the most likely time to see them.

Several companies run dolphin-spotting **boat trips** around the Moray Firth. However, researchers claim that the increased traffic is causing the dolphins unnecessary stress, particularly during the all-important breeding period when passing vessels are thought to force calves underwater for uncomfortably long periods. So if you decide to go on a cruise to see the dolphins, which also sometimes provides the chance of spotting minke whales, porpoises, seals and otters, make sure that the operator is a member of the Dolphin Space Programme's accreditation scheme (www.dolphinspace.org).

BOAT TOURS

Trips with these accredited operators, most of which operate between April and October, are especially popular in July and August, so be sure to book them well in advance.

Ecoventures Victoria Place, Cromarty; www.ecoventures.co.uk. Based in Cromarty on the Black Isle, Ecoventures run 2hr wildlife cruises (from £36) with the chance to spot dolphins, harbour porpoises and grey seals.

Phoenix Sea Adventures www.phoenix-nairn.co.uk. Runs 2hr trips from Findhorn and Lossiemouth (from £40).

1

maltings. The slick and informative tour begins with a look around an exhibition area, before setting off for a guided walk around the impressive distillery. The bubbling 100,000-litre washbacks and sparkling copper wash stills show how advances in technology have streamlined the distilling process, while an old customs office and preserved kilns from the original building bring alive the history of the operation. The tour culminates in a generous tasting session, including drams of the Singleton of Glen Ord.

Fortrose and Rosemarkie

FORTROSE, ten miles northeast of Inverness, is a quietly elegant village dominated by the beautiful ruins of a once huge, early thirteenth-century **cathedral** (daily 9.30am–5.30pm; free) founded by King David I. It languishes on a pretty green bordered by red-sandstone and colourwashed houses. One mile beyond, **ROSEMARKIE** is equally appealing, with its neat high street of stone houses. On sunny days local families descend on the sandy beach, where a cheap-and-cheerful café has picnic benches looking out to sea.

Groam House Museum

High St, Rosemarkie • April–Oct Mon–Fri 11am–4.30pm, Sat 2–4.30pm; Nov to early Dec Sat 2–4pm • Free • https://groamhouse.org.uk

At the lower end of Rosemarkie's high street, **Groam House Museum** displays fifteen intricately carved **Pictish standing stones** (among them the famous Rosemarkie Cross Slab) dating from as early as the eighth century. An informative video highlights other sites in a region that was a stronghold of Pictish culture – a primer to tempt any history buff into a visit to Portmahomack (see page 43). There's also a harp to pluck, and kids can "build their own" digital Rosemarkie Stone and print it out.

Cromarty

An appealing jumble of handsome Georgian townhouses and pretty workers' cottages knitted together by a cat's-cradle of lanes, **CROMARTY**, the Black Isle's main settlement, is simply a joy to wander around and well worth the detour from the designated North Coast 500 route. An ancient ferry crossing on the pilgrimage trail to Tain, it became a prominent port in 1772, fuelling a period of prosperity that gave Cromarty some of the Highlands' finest Georgian houses. The railways poached that trade in the nineteenth century – a branch line to the town was begun but never completed – but the flip side of stagnation is preservation. While in Cromarty, be sure to drop into **Hugh Miller's Birthplace Cottage and Museum** (Church St; late March to Sept daily noon–5pm; free, donations welcome; NTS; www.nts.org.uk), the thatched home of Cromarty's celebrated social reformer.

ACCOMMODATION AND EATING   CROMARTY

★ **The Factor's House** Denny Rd; www.thefactors house.com. Hosts Fiona and Graham go the extra mile at their luxury B&B. King-size beds, roll-top baths and fluffy bathrobes await in the three rooms – the Urquhart is our pick – while the lounge is a peaceful spot for a drink by the fire. Featuring fresh Scottish cuisine and home-baked delights, the dinner menu has been awarded an AA rosette and a nod from the Michelin Guide. **££**

Sutor Creek 21 Bank St; www.sutorcreek.co.uk. A lovely café-restaurant full of laidback seaside charm. It focuses on local and seasonal food, whether light lunches (£6–10) or excellent dinners like Shetland scallops with black pudding. The same ethos carries into wood-fired pizzas, best washed down with Cromarty Brewery beers. A gem. May–Sept daily 10am–8pm; Oct–April Wed–Sun 10–8pm. **£**

Strathpeffer and around

Visitors first came to this leafy Victorian spa town to take the waters, then in the 1970s and 1980s they arrived on coach tours to wallow in its faded glamour. Now **STRATHPEFFER** is restyling itself again as a place for activities in the surrounding hills, with a focus – ironically – on "wellbeing" that sees it return to its origins as a renowned

European **health resort**. All manner of guests disembarked from the *Strathpeffer Spa Express* train: George Bernard Shaw, Emmeline Pankhurst (who caused a scandal with a lecture on women's rights) and Franklin and Eleanor Roosevelt on honeymoon.

Renovation has transformed the town's Victorian grand hall into an arts centre and upgraded the adjacent **Upper Pump Room** (April–Sept Mon–Sat 10am–5pm, Sun 1–5pm; donation), where displays narrate the spa town's fascinating history.

Rogie Falls

The **Rogie Falls** lie two miles north of the village of Contin, on the main A835 to Braemore. They're well signposted and it's a five-minute walk from the car park to where the Black Water froths down a stretch of rocks and mini-gorges, in one place plunging 26ft. Salmon leap upriver in high summer, particularly at a fish ladder built next to the toughest rapids. A suspension bridge over the river leads to some waymarked forest trails, including a five-mile loop to View Rock, at a point only 160ft above sea level, but which has great views of the local area.

ACCOMMODATION   STRATHPEFFER AND AROUND

Coul House Hotel Contin, 2 miles south of Strathpeffer, https://coulhousehotel.com. Expect a very warm welcome at this beautiful 1820s mansion in the village of Contin, which offers a traditional Highlands experience with modern conveniences. Views from the elegant rooms look out over the gardens – the finest with four-poster beds are worth the splash for a special occasion – while the lounge areas have crackling fires, leather-bound books and chessboards. The ornately decorated, octagonal restaurant serves exquisite Scottish cuisine like venison steak or veggie options such as pan-fried falafel. Rates significantly cheaper out of high season. **££££**

Dingwall and around

The modest wee town of **DINGWALL** has long been bypassed, with most drivers preferring the quicker and more direct A9. Admittedly there's not a great deal to keep you here, although while in the area it's worth stopping by the impressive hilltop **Macdonald Monument**, dedicated to the son of a local crofter who fought in the Boer War. The town is also home to the community-owned **GlenWyvis Distillery** (https://glenwyvis.com), a refreshing alternative to the behemoth distillery operations in the Highlands, whose 2600 investors made it one of the UK's largest ever crowd-funded projects. The craft distillery, entirely powered by renewable energy, released its first single malt in 2021. To buy a bottle of its renowned single malt or one of the excellent GlenWyvis gins, stop by the Highland Farm Café (see below) just up the road at Mountgerald.

OUTDOOR ACTIVITIES   DINGWALL AND AROUND

Trout Quest Evanton, 7 miles north of Dingwall; www.troutquest.com. The friendly guides at Trout Quest offer expert guidance on their fly fishing day trips and longer fishing holidays. Crash-course beginners' lessons teach how to fly fish for trout and salmon, with all equipment included, and they also offer boat hire and trout permits for several local lochs: contact Trout Quest for prices.

EATING

Highland Farm Café Mountgerald; https://highlandfarmcafe.co.uk. This wee eco-café serves seasonal Scottish dishes like handmade Highland beef burgers and veggie haggis jacket potato melts at wallet-friendly prices. There's also a gift shop-cum-community larder stocked with local snacks, drinks and trinkets, while the outdoor play area will keep kids entertained. An excellent pit stop before travels north. Year-round, daily 9am–5pm. **£**

The Storehouse of Foulis Foulis Ferry, Evanton; https://thestorehouse.scot. This self-service restaurant makes a pleasant lunch stop on the road north. Expect hearty portions of lasagne, chicken casserole, plus gluten-free and meat-free options like their piri-piri vegetable stew (all around £8). The menu changes daily and features local produce. Grab a seat by the window and look out for the seals in the Cromarty Firth. There's also a visitor centre and shop. Mon–Sat 9am–5pm. **££**

The road to John O'Groats

For many, the eighty-mile coastal road from the Dornoch Firth to John O'Groats signifies the end of a long journey. But for those embarking on the North Coast 500, the adventure has only just begun. As you travel from East Sutherland into Caithness, the landscape is dominated by verdant, rolling farmland to the left and never-ending sea views to the right; a few hundred miles away, the southern tip of Norway hides out of sight. The climate in these parts is generally sunnier and drier than in the west, allowing for pleasant wanders around the handsome villages that dot the route, while a few blockbuster historic buildings – Dunrobin Castle, Dornoch Cathedral and Castle Sinclair Girnigoe – are among the most interesting architectural sights in the Highlands.

HIGHLIGHTS

❶ **Dornoch** Genteel Dornoch has emerged as something of an upmarket resort, with its boutique shops, world-class golf course and the odd celebrity sighting. See page 44

❷ **Dunrobin Castle** This opulent pile looks like it comes straight from a fairytale; visit late morning or early afternoon for the falconry displays. See page 45

❸ **Time-travelling at Timespan Heritage Centre** This excellent museum brings the area's colourful history to life – from the

Vikings to the Clearances – with hi-tech displays. See page 46

❹ **Go on a RIB adventure** Take an exhilarating tour aboard a Rigid Inflatable Boat from Wick harbour. The trips take in castles, sea stacks and caves, with the chance of spotting puffins and seals. See page 49

❺ **Castle Sinclair Girnigoe** Perched improbably on a cliff-edge, this crumbling old royal pile – now populated by chattering seabirds – is the most captivating ruin on the east coast. See page 49

2

The main route across the **Dornoch Firth** takes in some handsome old towns, like **Tain** and **Dornoch**, although those with more time on their hands should take a detour to **Portmahomack** for its towering lighthouse, **Bonar Bridge** for mountain biking adventures, **Carbisdale Castle** for forest trails, waterfalls and the 1650 Battle of Carbisdale site, or the **Falls of Shin** for the leaping salmon. Travelling north, the story of the Clearances – ruthlessly pursued by the Sutherland family of Dunrobin Castle – is told through a series of heritage centres in **Helmsdale**, **Dunbeath** and **Wick**. Whisky aficionados are likely to enjoy this leg, too, with distillery tours and tasting sessions available at Glenmorangie, Clynelish and Old Pulteney.

GETTING AROUND | **THE ROAD TO JOHN O'GROATS**

From the Dornoch Firth to John O'Groats, the North Coast 500 follows the exhilarating coastal A9 road. **Drivers**, **motorcyclists** and **larger vehicles** have little to think about on this straight road, interrupted by the occasional 20 or 30mph restriction through villages, until you reach Latheron, where the A9 forks left to Thurso and the North Coast 500 continues on the A99 to Wick. **Cyclists** have no choice but to keep to the same route as drivers, with ascents before Helmsdale and Berriedale. North of Wick, the terrain plateaus on the road to John O'Groats; drivers should remember to give the obligatory waves of support to the heavily laden cyclists completing their long journeys from Land's End.

The Dornoch Firth and around

For centuries, visitors on the pilgrim trail to the **Fearn peninsula** came from the south by ferry from Cromarty. Nowadays the area north of **Dornoch Firth** is linked by the A9, skirting past the quiet town of **Tain**, best known as the home of Glenmorangie whisky, and the neat town of **Dornoch** itself, an unexpected pleasure known for its cathedral and golf courses.

Tain

There's a sense of having arrived somewhere as you swing through central **TAIN** with its handsome buildings. Reputedly Scotland's oldest Royal Burgh, it was the birthplace of **St Duthus**, an eleventh-century missionary. Many a medieval pilgrim came to venerate his miracle-working relics enshrined first in a sanctuary then in fourteenth-century **St Duthus Collegiate Church**. James IV visited annually, usually fresh from the arms of his mistress, Janet Kennedy, whom he had installed in nearby Moray.

THE ROAD TO JOHN O'GROATS

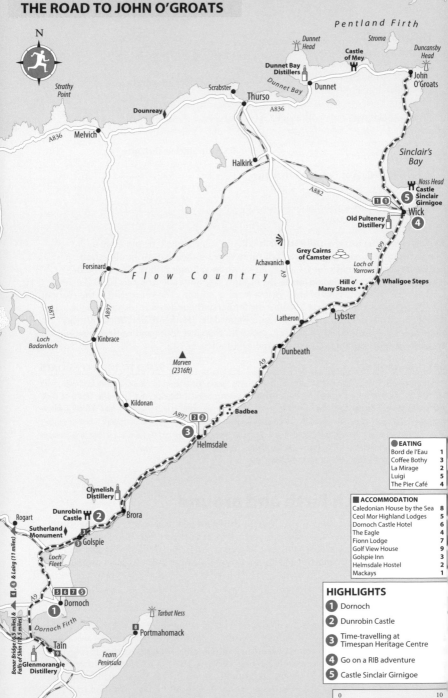

N

Pentland Firth

Dunnet Head

Stroma

Duncansby Head

Castle of Mey

Dunnet

John O'Groats

Dunnet Bay Distillers

Dunnet Bay

Scrabster

Thurso

A836

Dounreay

Strathy Point

A836

Melvich

Halkirk

Sinclair's Bay

A882

Noss Head

Castle Sinclair Girnigoe ❺

Wick ❹

Old Pulteney Distillery

Forsinard

Flow Country

Achavanich

Grey Cairns of Camster

Loch of Yarrows

Hill o' Many Stanes

Whaligoe Steps

B871

A897

Kinbrace

Loch Badanloch

Latheron

Lybster

A9

Morven (2316ft)

Dunbeath

Kildonan

A897

Badbea

❸ Helmsdale

Clynelish Distillery

Dunrobin Castle ❷ Brora

Rogart

Sutherland Monument

Golspie ❸

Loch Fleet

Bonar Bridge (6.5 miles) & Falls of Shin (11.5 miles)

A9

❺❻❼❺ Dornoch ❶

Tarbat Ness

Dornoch Firth

Tain

Portmahomack

Glenmorangie Distillery

Fearn Peninsula

🔴 **EATING**
Bord de l'Eau	1
Coffee Bothy	3
La Mirage	2
Luigi	5
The Pier Café	4

⬛ **ACCOMMODATION**
Caledonian House by the Sea	8
Ceol Mor Highland Lodges	5
Dornoch Castle Hotel	6
The Eagle	4
Fionn Lodge	7
Golf View House	9
Golspie Inn	3
Helmsdale Hostel	2
Mackays	1

HIGHLIGHTS

❶ Dornoch

❷ Dunrobin Castle

❸ Time-travelling at Timespan Heritage Centre

❹ Go on a RIB adventure

❺ Castle Sinclair Girnigoe

0 ——————— 10
miles

Glenmorangie Distillery

On the A9, 1 mile northwest of Tain • Tours June–Aug daily 10am–4pm every 30min, April–May & Sept–Oct Mon–Sat 10am–3pm hourly, Nov–March 10am or 2pm by appointment; shop Mon–Fri 10am–5pm, April–Oct also Sat 10am–4pm, June–Aug also Sun noon–4pm • Charge (book ahead) • www.glenmorangie.com

Tain's most popular attraction is the **Glenmorangie Distillery**. Tours of the whisky distillery and warehouses explain the alchemic process that ferments mashed malt, distils the liquid in Scotland's tallest stills then matures it in oak casks to create a delicate, vanilla-y malt. There's a dram or two to finish, naturally. Die-hard whisky aficionados should consider the more comprehensive tasting session on the Signet Tour.

2

ACCOMMODATION   TAIN

Golf View House 13 Knockbreck Rd; https://bedand breakfasttain.co.uk. Just south of Tain centre, this former manse with five bedrooms offers a lovely B&B stay. The decor is relaxed, contemporary Scottish with a touch of romance and the en-suite bathrooms are excellent. Factor in fine views to the Dornoch Firth and a full Scottish breakfast, too. **££**

Portmahomack and around

The fishing village of **PORTMAHOMACK**, strung out around a curving sandy beach, is a surprise after the rolling fields of the **Fearn peninsula** east of Tain. Though all but empty nowadays, this was a heartland of eighth-century Picts before the Viking raids became too much.

Tarbat Ness

North of Portmahomack lies **Tarbat Ness**, a gorse-covered point with one of the Britain's tallest lighthouses at its tip. Come for sea views and a seven-mile stroll (2–3hr round trip). The **walk** heads south from Tarbat Ness for three miles, following a narrow passage between the cliffs and foreshore, to the hamlet of Rockfield. A road leads past fishermen's cottages to Portmahomack to rejoin the road back to the lighthouse.

ACCOMMODATION   PORTMAHOMACK AND AROUND

Caledonian House by the Sea Main St, Portmahomack; www.caledonian-house.co.uk. This lovely B&B opened in 2015. The en-suite rooms, all on the upper floor, have enormous beds, and there are excellent sea views from the breakfast room. A beachfront woodcraft, jewellery and art gallery enhances the offering. Gallery open Fri–Sun 11.30am–3.30pm or by appointment. **£**

Bonar Bridge

The A9 across the Kyle of Sutherland has left **BONAR BRIDGE** out on a limb. Yet in the fifteenth century this was a heart of the region's industry because of a large iron foundry. James IV passed through and was so shocked to find the forest virtually clear-felled that he ordered oak saplings to be planted – the ancient woodland east of Bonar Bridge dates from this era. Several miles of **mountain-biking trails** run through nearby Forestry Commission woodland, with blue and black grade trails at Balblair two miles north, and blue and red trails beneath Carbisdale Castle, although the latter have been decommissioned and are therefore no longer maintained.

Lairg and around

North of Bonar Bridge, the A836 parallels the River Shin to **LAIRG**, scattered at the eastern end of **Loch Shin**. Lairg and its surrounds are growing in popularity as a base for slowing down and enjoying attractions inland. Its fairly central location allows for day-trips to any corner of the route, with nowhere more than 90 minutes away. The **Wee Hoose** on Little Loch Shin provides a comical photo opportunity once you read the backstory on the nearby information board, while **The Pier Café**, with locally sourced ingredients and panoramic views across the loch, comes highly rated. Lairg's annual lamb sale in mid-August is one of Europe's largest one-day markets.

Falls of Shin
4 miles south of Lairg

A reason to come this way is the **Falls of Shin** in Achany Glen: one of the best places in Scotland to see **salmon** leap on their upstream migration between March and November; the 12ft cascade is on the cusp of the maximum leap for a fish and most tumble back into the river. There's a visitor centre with a café, a playpark and a gift shop.

ACTIVITIES
LAIRG AND AROUND

Connell Outdoor Pursuits www.connelloutdoor pursuits.com. From the comfort of a warm pickup truck, head off on one of Kurt Connell's state-of-the-art nighttime thermal imaging safaris. When the deer, pine martens, badgers, foxes and rabbits come out to play, you'll take the camera controls and carefully observe from a distance; zooming in and panning around to see what roams around Lairg. Ideal for those who don't have luck spotting wildlife or want a unique perspective on the Highlands at night. Kurt will pick you up from your accommodation around Lairg or Bonar Bridge; deer sightings guaranteed. £75pp.

ACCOMMODATION AND EATING
LAIRG AND AROUND

★ **Ceol Mor Highland Lodges** 7 miles south of Lairg; www.ceolmor.co.uk. Opened in 2022, these eco-friendly lodges tick all the boxes for the perfect self-catered North Coast 500 base. Both lodges overlook the peaceful Kyle of Sutherland, kitchens are well-equipped and pine martens are regular visitors. Hosts Alan and Yvonne are passionate about the area and more than happy to help plan adventures. 7-night minimum stay. **££**

The Pier Café Lochside, Lairg; www.pier-cafe.co.uk. Opened in 2010, The Pier is a popular hub for locals and is often booked up on weekends, so book well ahead. Hearty soups plus locally caught fish feature in this reasonably priced restaurant with excellent views. Mon–Sat 10am– 4pm, Fri & Sat also 5.30–9pm, Sun 10am–6pm. **££**

Dornoch

DORNOCH, a genteel, villagey town eight miles north of Tain, lies on a headland overlooking the **Dornoch Firth**. Blessed with good looks and a sunny climate (by Scottish standards) and surrounded by sand dunes, it has morphed into a modest upmarket resort: all antiques shops and fine accommodation in the historic sandstone centre, a championship **golf course** plus miles of sandy beaches just outside. The town had its fifteen minutes of fame in 2002, when Madonna married Guy Ritchie at nearby **Skibo Castle** and had her son baptized in Dornoch Cathedral.

The Cathedral
Castle St • Visitor times mid-May to mid-Sept Mon–Fri 10am–4pm; services Sun 11am • www.dornoch-cathedral.com

Dating from the twelfth century, Dornoch became a royal burgh in 1628. Pride of place among its oldest buildings grouped around the square is the imposing **Cathedral**, founded in 1224 and built of local sandstone. The original was horribly damaged by marauding Mackays in 1570, and much of what you see today was restored by the Countess of Sutherland in 1835, though the worst of her Victorian excesses were removed in the twentieth century, when the interior stonework was returned to its original state. The stained-glass windows in the north wall were later additions. The counterpart to the cathedral is the fortified sixteenth-century **Bishop's Palace** opposite, now refurbished as a hotel (see below).

INFORMATION
DORNOCH

Tourist office This tourist information centre on Argyll St near the *Dornoch Castle Hotel* (Mon–Fri 10am–2pm; 07341 284405) has a section devoted to the North Coast 500.

ACCOMMODATION AND EATING

★**Dornoch Castle Hotel** Castle St; https:// dornochcastlehotel.com. For a splurge, choose the fabulous historic deluxe rooms in the turreted tower of the Bishop's Palace. Elsewhere this smart hotel is more modern – spacious superior rooms with pillow chocolates and whisky miniatures, or comfy but bland garden-facing rooms. There's an in-house whisky micro-distillery and a single malt bar; it's no surprise that Dornoch Castle was recently voted Scotland's best whisky hotel. Bar food served daily noon–3pm; restaurant daily 6.30–9pm. **££££**

The Eagle Castle St; 01862 810008. Dornoch's first bar with rooms, specialising in whiskies, real ales and filling Sunday lunches. Rooms are modern and comfortable, and breakfast is plentiful. Book early as there are only nine rooms. Food served Mon–Sun noon–9pm. **£**

Luigi Castle St; 01862 810893. A modern metropolitan-styled bistro focuses on soups, ciabattas and pizzas during the day, and in the evenings serves seafood dishes such as mussels in red Thai broth. Lunch daily 11am–2pm; dinner Easter–Oct Sat & Sun 6.45–9pm, & daily during peak months. **£££**

North to Wick

North of Dornoch, the A9 hugs the coast for most of the sixty miles to **Wick**, the principal settlement in the far north of the mainland. The most telling landmark in the stretch is the **Sutherland Monument** near Golspie, erected to the first duke of Sutherland, the landowner who oversaw the eviction of thousands of tenants during the Clearances. That bitter memory haunts the small towns and villages of this stretch, including **Brora**, **Dunbeath**, **Lybster** and pretty **Helmsdale**. Nonetheless, many of these settlements went on to flourish through a thriving fishing trade, none more so than Wick, once the busiest herring port in Europe.

Golspie and around

Ten miles north of Dornoch the North Coast 500 rolls through the red-sandstone town of **GOLSPIE**. It's a pleasantly bustling if fairly forgettable place, and for most visitors serves only as a gateway to good mountain-bike trails (www.highlandwildcat. com) or the grandest castle of this coastline.

The Sutherland Monument

Approaching Golspie, you can't miss the **monument** to the first duke of Sutherland on the summit of **Beinn a'Bhragaidh** (Ben Bhraggie). A 30ft-high statue on a 79ft column, it bears an inscription which recalls its creation in 1834 by "a mourning and grateful tenantry [to] a judicious, kind and liberal landlord", and quietly overlooks the fact that the duke forcibly evicted fifteen thousand crofters from his million-acre estate. The stiff **climb** to the monument (round trip 1hr 30min) provides vast coast views, but the steep path is tough going and there's little view until the top. Head up Fountain Road and pass (or park at) Rhives Farm, then pick up signs for the Beinn a'Bhragaidh footpath (BBFP).

Dunrobin Castle

A9, 1 mile north of Golspie • May, June, July, Aug & Sept 10am–5pm; Apr & Oct 10.30am–4.30pm • Charge • http://dunrobincastle.co.uk

The largest house in the Highlands and modelled on a Loire chateau, **Dunrobin Castle** was designed by Sir Charles Barry, the architect behind London's Houses of Parliament. It is the seat of the Sutherland family, once Europe's biggest landowners with a staggering 1.3 million acres. They were also the driving force behind the Clearances here – it's worth remembering that such extravagance was paid for by evicting thousands of crofters.

Tours of the **interior** visit only a tenth of the 189 furnished rooms, which are as opulent as you'd expect with their fine furniture, paintings (including works by Edwin Landseer, Allan Ramsay and Sir Joshua Reynolds), tapestries and objets d'art. Alongside, providing a venue for falconry displays (11.30am & 2pm), the attractive **gardens** are pleasant to wander en route to Dunrobin's **museum**, housed in the former summerhouse and the repository of the Sutherlands' vulgar hunting trophies – heads and horns on the walls plus displays of everything from elephants' toes to rhinos' tails – and ethnographic holiday souvenirs from Africa.

The last extravagance is that the castle has its own **train** station (summer only) on the Inverness–Wick line; no surprise, considering that the duke built the railway.

Clynelish Distillery

Clynelish Road, Brora • Tours daily, 10.30am & 1.30pm; fewer tours in autumn/winter – visit website for details • Charge • http://malts.com/en-row/distilleries/clynelish

The first distillery on this site started producing whisky in 1819, and continued until the late 1960s when the more modern **Clynelish Distillery** began production. Today, it has a reputation for producing floral, waxy whiskies and has close connections with Johnnie Walker Gold Label Reserve.

ACCOMMODATION AND EATING — **GOLSPIE AND AROUND**

Coffee Bothy Fountain Rd, Golspie; 01408 633022. A cabin-style café popular with bikers and walkers. Fill up on all-day breakfasts, fresh soups and ciabattas, then reward yourself a home-baked treat afterwards. Feb–Dec Mon–Sat 9am–4pm. £̄

Golspie Inn Old Bank Road, Golspie; www.golspieinn. co.uk. Two-hundred-year-old hotel and restaurant a mile-or-so from Dunrobin Castle. Rooms were refurbished in 2021 and are subsequently more modern than many similarly priced hotels along the A9. Excellent value, even in high-season. £̄£̄

Helmsdale

HELMSDALE is one of the largest villages between Golspie and Wick, and it's certainly the most picturesque: a tight little grid of streets set above a river-mouth harbour. Romantic novelist Barbara Cartland was a frequent visitor and must have looked as exotic as a flamingo in its grey stone streets. For all its charm, it's a newcomer, founded in the nineteenth century to house the evicted inhabitants of Strath Kildonan, which lies behind it, and which subsequently flourished as a herring port.

Timespan Heritage Centre

Dunrobin St • March–Oct daily Mon–Sat & Sun 10am–5pm; Nov–March Tues noon–4pm, Sat & Sun 10am–3pm • Charge • https://timespan.org.uk

Good looks and sleepy ambience aside, the appeal of Helmsdale is the **Timespan Heritage Centre** beside the river. An ambitious venture for a place this size, the modern museum tells the story of Viking raids, the Kildonan Gold Rush and the Clearances; it also explores crofting in re-created houses, and fishing through high-tech displays, with a movement sensor to navigate animations of local yarns. There's an art gallery-and-café, too, serving up soups and cakes, with lovely views out to the river.

ACCOMMODATION AND EATING — **HELMSDALE**

Helmsdale Hostel Stafford St; https://helmsdalehostel.co.uk. Run by host Irene, this wee hostel sleeps fourteen guests in two dorms and two rooms. Easter–Sept; entire property available out of season. £̄

La Mirage Dunrobin St; https://lamirage.co.uk. Not quite "The North's Premier Restaurant" as it claims, but possibly the most bizarre due to the tastes in decor of a former proprietor who styled herself after Barbara Cartland. The menu, although as dated as Babs herself, is solid: locally caught haddock and chips, gammon steaks, even onion ring stacks. Daily 11am–9pm. £̄£̄

Dunbeath and around

The landscape becomes wilder north of Helmsdale. Once over the long haul up the **Ord of Caithness** – a steep hill which used to be a major obstacle and is still blocked by

snowstorms – the scenery switches from heather-clad moors to treeless grazing lands, dotted with derelict crofts and dry-stone walls.

Dunbeath

DUNBEATH was another village founded to provide work in the wake of the Clearances, laid along the glen beside the river. The local landlord built a harbour at the river mouth in 1800, at the start of the herring boom, and the settlement briefly flourished. It now suffers the indignity of an A9 flyover soaring over much of the village.

The novelist Neil Gunn was born in one of the terraced houses beneath the flyover and his tale is told in the **Dunbeath Heritage Museum** (April–Sept Mon–Wed 10am–5pm, same hours 1st & 3rd Sat, Sun 11am–4pm, call ahead Thurs–Fri and in winter; www.dunbeath-heritage.org.uk), alongside exhibits of local Pictish and Viking history, plus a painted river on the floor featuring quotes from Gunn's *Highland River*.

Lybster and around

Another neat planned village, **LYBSTER** (pronounced "libe-ster") was established at the height of the nineteenth-century herring boom. Two hundred boats once worked out of its picturesque small harbour, a story told in the **Waterlines** heritage centre at Lybster Harbour, May–Oct daily 11am–5pm; small donation requested, 01593 721520) – there are modern displays about the "silver darlings" and the fishermen who pursued them, plus a smokehouse and a café.

Seven miles north of Lybster, the **Grey Cairns of Camster** are the most impressive of the prehistoric burial sites that litter this stretch of coast. Surrounded by moorland, these two enormous reconstructed burial chambers were originally built five thousand years ago with corbelled dry-stone roofs in their hidden chambers. A few miles further north on the A99, the 365 uneven **Whaligoe Steps** lead steeply down to a natural harbour surrounded by high cliffs. A beautiful summer sunset spot.

Wick and around

Since it was founded by Vikings as *Vik* (meaning "bay"), **WICK** has lived by the sea. It's actually two towns: Wick proper and, south across the river, **Pultneytown**, created by the British Fisheries Society in 1806 to encourage evicted crofters to take up fishing. By the mid-nineteenth century, Wick was the busiest herring port in Europe, with a fleet of more than 1100 boats exporting fish to Russia, Scandinavia and the West Indian slave plantations. The demise of its fishing trade has left Wick down at heel, reduced to a mere transport hub. Yet the huge harbour in Pultneytown and a walk around the surrounding area – scruffy rows of fishermen's cottages, derelict net-mending sheds and stores – gives an insight into the scale of the former fishing trade.

Wick Heritage Centre

Bank Row, Pultneytown • Easter–Oct Mon–Sat 10am–5pm, last entry 3.45pm • Charge • https://wickheritage.org

The volunteer-maintained **Wick Heritage Centre** is the best place to evoke the heyday of the fishing boom. Deceptively labyrinthine, it contains a fascinating array of artefacts from the old days, including fully rigged boats, models of the sea-faring vessels and reconstructed period rooms, plus a superb archive of photographs from the Johnstone Collection captured by three generations of a local family between 1863 and 1975.

Old Pulteney Distillery

Huddart St • May–Sept Mon–Sat 10am–5pm; Oct–April Mon–Fri 10am–4pm • Tours at 11am & 2pm or by arrangement • Charge • http://oldpulteney.com

Until the city fathers declared Wick dry in the 1920s, the fishermen consumed three hundred gallons of whisky a day. The last distillery in town – and second most northerly in Scotland – distils more refined malts nowadays; most are light or medium-bodied, with a hint of sea salt. The tours give a close-up glimpse of a functioning distillery, which is less polished than some of the others in the Highlands and more charming for it. Needless to say, it ends with a dram or full tastings.

Castle Sinclair Girnigoe

Noss Head, 4 miles north of Wick. Leave the town on Broadhaven Rd towards Papigoe. At the next hamlet of Staxigoe, turn left at the T-junction then follow the road for 2 miles. The castle is a short walk signposted from the car park.

It's unlikely you'll stumble across **Castle Sinclair Girnigoe** by mistake, located as it is down a long unsigned road, but seek it out and the rewards are great. The cliff-side castle, with perpendicular sides that tower fifty feet high, is thought to have been built in the fourteenth century, although some archaeologists believe the site has been occupied for thousands of years thanks to its strategic position. Today, the castle is a shell of its former glory, home to hundreds of seabirds whose squawks echo around the old Tower House. After wandering around the captivating ruins, walk down the dry moat to the rocky inlet, or "goe". One of the best spots on the North Coast 500 to photograph the aurora borealis, or northern lights.

2

ACTIVITIES   WICK AND AROUND

Caithness Sea Coast www.caithness-seacoast.co.uk. 30min Wick harbour cruises plus longer tours to spot wildlife and admire the high cliffs in a fast RIB boat. The operator also runs longer, 3hr trips to Lybster, and one-way trips in either direction. From £23. April–Oct.

ACCOMMODATION AND EATING

Bord de l'Eau Market St; 01955 604400. This riverside bistro offers a slice of France, with a changing menu of Gaelic and seafood dishes, plus some French classics. The best seats are in the airy conservatory. Tues–Sat noon–2.30pm & 6–9pm, dinner only Sun. **£££**

★ **Mackays** Union St; www.mackayshotel.co.uk. Plush beds, streamlined oak furnishings and a prominent corner position on the world's shortest street (yes, really) make this Wick's prime accommodation option. Book the superior twin/king for excellent views over the Wick River. Its acclaimed *No.1 Bistro* serves superb scallops and beef, plus a stellar fish and chips. Lunch and dinner Mon noon–10.30pm, Tues noon–11pm, Weds 2–11pm, Thurs–Sun noon–11pm. **££**

Along the north coast

The journey from John O'Groats to Durness, along mainland Britain's northernmost road, brings a dramatic transformation of landscape. The scenery shifts from the sleepy sheep-grazed farmland of Caithness to the rugged, maroon heathland of Sutherland, with views of the tooth-like pinnacles of Ben Hope and Ben Loyal offering a sneak preview of the cinematic landscape that awaits in Assynt and Wester Ross. While driving, keep half an eye out for the gorgeous, deserted white-sand beaches that become more regular the further west you travel; there are two divine spots near Bettyhill. If you're taking things slow, and fancy a breather from the main North Coast 500 route, take a detour inland to the vast Flow Country, where you can book onto a guided tour of the peat bogs, unique to Scotland.

HIGHLIGHTS

❶ Duncansby Head sea stacks
Razorbills, puffins and kittiwakes flit in prolific numbers at these imposing sea stacks, near a lighthouse that marks the northeastern point of mainland Britain. See below

❷ Castle of Mey The royal heritage of this sixteenth-century pile lives on today: it was the late Queen Mother's holiday home for almost fifty years and is still visited by the now King Charles, who comes up for the Mey Highland Games. See page 53

❸ Surfing in Thurso Surfers congregate in Thurso for "Thurso East", one of the most powerful breaks in Europe. To enjoy the culture without the peril, hang out at the *Thurso Community Café*. See page 54

❹ Explore the Flow Country The world's "biggest blanket bog" may not seem appealing, but the birdlife and trail walks in the Flow Country make it well worth the detour. See page 57

❺ Crossing the Kyle of Tongue Don't even think about missing out on the photo opportunities from the causeway that crosses the Kyle of Tongue, where the peaks of Ben Hope and Ben Loyal loom in the distance. See page 57

3

While many visitors to **John O'Groats** take a selfie by the iconic sign, then head straight off, there are a number of sights close by that warrant a longer stay in the area, not least Scotland's most northerly whisky distillery, **8 Doors** (www.8doorsdistillery.com), which opened in 2022, complete with a visitor centre, whisky lounge and café. Tours and tasting sessions are available.

The **Duncansby Head** stacks teem with seabirds on their migration south, while the view from **Dunnet Head** – mainland Britain's northernmost point – offers a wonderful perspective across the entire north coast and out to Orkney. Those with an interest in British royalty should pay a visit to the **Castle of Mey**, while surfers will find it hard to resist the powerful waves in **Thurso**.

Heading west towards Durness, it's impossible to resist pulling into the car park on the causeway that crosses the **Kyle of Tongue**, where, to the south, epic mountain views glimmer behind the golden sand banks.

GETTING AROUND   **ALONG THE NORTH COAST**

The coastal A836 road west of John O'Groats snakes between a string of wee villages, with Thurso offering the best chance for **drivers** and **motorcyclists** to pick up supplies and fill up on petrol. Strictly speaking it's 60mph along most of the north coast (except through the built-up settlements), but the twists and turns – let alone the views – mean you should take it slow. Around Loch Eriboll you will encounter your first sustained single-track road; look ahead and check behind for oncoming vehicles, and use the passing places accordingly (see page 23). **Camper vans** and **caravans** should treat this as practice for the even wigglier roads that lie ahead in Assynt and Wester Ross. **Cyclists** will find this stretch hillier than the east coast, with a serious climb shortly after Bettyhill and a relentless ascent from sea level to 728ft out of Tongue – both are rewarded with eye-watering downhills shortly afterwards.

John O'Groats and around

Snap-happy tourists, windswept pilgrims and exhausted cyclists convene at **JOHN O'GROATS**, the most northeasterly settlement on mainland Britain. Consisting of a car park, a souvenir village and not much else, the place has never quite lived up to its folkloric name, although a recent regeneration project has brought some new life to the place with the opening of a technicolour seafront hotel and a café.

There are plenty of prettier places to view the sea in north Scotland, but as one end of the Land's End to John O'Groats tour, it always brimming with a happy flow of people either starting or ending a life-affirming journey here.

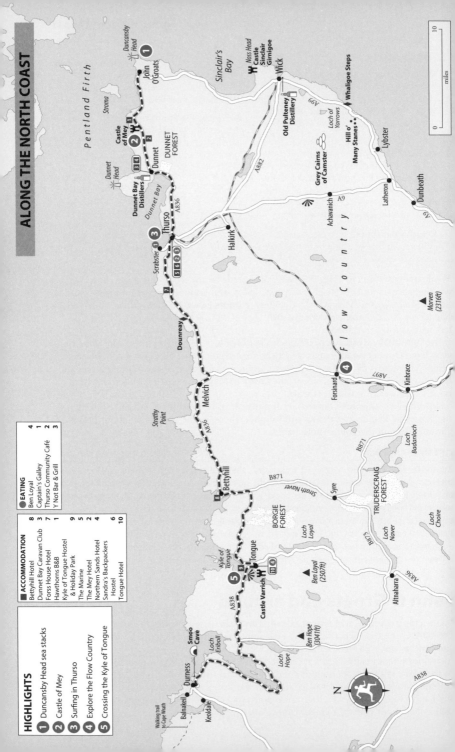

ALONG THE NORTH COAST

HIGHLIGHTS

1. Duncansby Head sea stacks
2. Castle of Mey
3. Surfing in Thurso
4. Explore the Flow Country
5. Crossing the Kyle of Tongue

■ ACCOMMODATION

Bettyhill Hotel	8
Dunnet Bay Caravan Club	3
Forss House Hotel	1
Hawthorns B&B	7
Kyle of Tongue Hostel & Holiday Park	9
The Marine	5
The Mey Hotel	2
Northern Sands Hotel	4
Sandra's Backpackers Hostel	6
Tongue Hotel	10

● EATING

Ben Loyal	4
Captain's Galley	1
Thurso Community Café	2
Y Not Bar & Grill	3

Pentland Firth

Duncansby Head 1

Stroma

John O'Groats

Noss Head
Castle Sinclair Girnigoe
Wick

Sinclair's Bay

Castle of Mey 2

Dunnet Head

Dunnet Bay Distillers

Dunnet

DUNNET FOREST

Dunnet Bay

Old Pulteney Distillery

A882

Loch of Yarrows

Grey Cairns of Camster

Hill o' Many Stanes

Whaligoe Steps

Lybster

Thurso 3

Scrabster

Halkirk

Achavanich

A9

Latheron

Dunbeath

A836

A9

Dounreay

Flow Country

Morven (2316ft)

Forsinard 4

A897

Kinbrace

Melvich

Strathy Point

A836

Loch Badanloch

TRUDERSCRAIG FOREST

Loch Choire

Bettyhill

B871

BORGIE FOREST

Strath Naver

Syre

B873

Loch Naver

A836

Altnaharra

Kyle of Tongue

Tongue 5

Loch Loyal

Ben Loyal (2507ft)

Castle Varrich

Ben Hope (3041ft)

Loch Eriboll

Loch Hope

Smoo Cave

Durness

Balnakeil

Keoldale

Walking trail to Cape Wrath

A838

N

0   10
miles

Duncansby Head

Marked by a lonely square-towered lighthouse and spectacular cliffs, **Duncansby Head** is the actual northeastern point of mainland Britain, and offers the edge-of-the-world experience that you might have hoped for at John O'Groats, two miles west. The birdlife here is prolific – fulmars, razorbills, puffins, guillemots and kittiwakes in their thousands – while south of the headland lie spectacular 200ft-high cliffs, cut by sheer-sided clefts known locally as *geos*, and several impressive sea stacks. Ask nicely at the John O' Groats tourist information office and somebody might be able to take you on a free guided tour.

Castle of Mey

6.5 miles west of John O'Groats · **Castle** May–July & mid-Aug to Sept daily 10.20am–4pm · Charge · **Grounds** Same months 10am–5pm (same hours for shop, tearoom and visitor centre) · Charge · www.castleofmey.org.uk

The handful of houses that make up the village of Mey whizz past in a moment – yet it was here that the late Queen Mother had her Scottish home. The original **Castle of Mey** was a sixteenth-century Z-plan affair, owned by the earls of Caithness until 1889: it was bought in a state of disrepair by the Queen Mother in 1952, the year her husband, George VI, died. She spent her summer holidays here each August, which may help explain why it's a modest wee place, unstuffy inside despite the facade that bristles with turrets. The walls are hung with works by local amateur artists and watercolours by the now King Charles (who still visits in late July, when it's closed for two weeks), and personal mementoes of the Queen Mum remain on show – guides are more than happy to explain their significance. The **gardens** outside are a lovely spot for an amble on a sunny day, not least for their views across the Pentland Firth.

3

INFORMATION

Tourist office Beside the main car park (Easter–Oct Mon– Fri 10am–4pm, https://caithness.org).

ACCOMMODATION AND EATING

The Mey Hotel Mey, 8 miles west of John o'Groats; https://meyhotel.co.uk. A simple but comfortable stay in a 19th-century coaching inn almost opposite the castle entrance; previously known as the Castle Arms Hotel. All rooms are en suite and the family-size rooms are good value. The restaurant prepares good pub grub such as local steak, and fish and chips. March–Oct. ££

Hawthorns B&B On the A836, www.meybandb.co.uk.

High-end B&B with superb sea views out to Hoy from the bedrooms and the airy breakfast/sitting area. Super-king beds and well-finished bathrooms, plus welcome mod-cons such as satellite wi-fi and Nespresso machines make this stand out from the competition on the north coast. Walk to the end of the road to see the wee sea stack. Also offers dining packages with transport to local restaurants. March–Oct. ££

Dunnet and around

Despite the publicity given to John O'Groats, the most northerly point of mainland Britain is actually **Dunnet Head** four miles north of the sleepy village of **DUNNET**. It's an evocative spot up at the Dunnet Head, covered in heather and bog and plummeting in red cliffs at the headland, marked by a Stevenson lighthouse – on a clear day, you'll see the whole north coast spread out before you from Cape Wrath to Duncansby Head. There are very few facilities in the village of Dunnet itself, beyond the **Northern Sands Hotel** and Britain's most northerly micro-distillery, the Dunnet Bay Distillers (see below), but its often blustery coastline attracts keen surfers and there are plenty of trails to follow in Dunnet Forest, mainland Britain's northernmost community woodland.

Dunnet Bay

Just south of Dunnet lies Dunnet Bay, a vast, golden beach backed by huge dunes. Surfers come for a smattering of reef breaks plus a beach break that offers shelter for beginners, depending on whereabouts on the bay you tuck in. At the northeast end of the bay, the **Seadrift Visitor and Ranger Centre** (May–June & Sept Mon, Tues, Thurs, Fri & Sun 2–5pm; July–Aug from 10.30am; free; 01847 821531) holds an exhibition about the fauna of the northwest coast and the ecology of its sand dunes. It also stocks information leaflets on local history and nature walks.

Dunnet Bay Distillers

On the A836 in Dunnet • May–Oct Mon–Fri 10am–4pm • 45min tour with tasting session • Charge • www.dunnetbaydistillers.co.uk

Since opening in 2014, **Dunnet Bay Distillers** has quickly acquired a loyal following and stack of awards for its superlative gin and vodka. Despite the roaring trade, this is still very much a family business, with the ceramic Rock Rose and Holy Grass Vodka bottles hand-filled, waxed and signed on-site by the family and friends of owners Martin and Claire. On the tour visitors are guided through the distilling process, with spirit-tastings and a glimpse of some of their new experimental flavours. It's all about provenance here: the botanicals, herbs and fruit that go into the spirits are grown in the front garden – rhubarbs, thyme, figs and all. Even the still is named Elizabeth, after the late Queen Mother who spent part of the year at the Castle of Mey nearby.

ACTIVITIES · WICK AND AROUND

Above and Beyond www.aboveandbeyondtours.co.uk. Caithness local Angela offers informative walks, bespoke driving tours and wellness packages; her excellent local knowledge and ability to meticulously plan an itinerary shines through. Walks from £30pp.

ACCOMMODATION AND EATING · DUNNET AND AROUND

★ **Northern Sands Hotel** Dunnet; www.northernsands.co.uk. Brilliantly refurbished modern double rooms sit above a restaurant and bar the locals rave about. Scottish favourites like Cullen skink and Scrabster haddock stand out on a menu revolving around local produce. You'd be hard pressed to find a better value hotel with breakfast included on the north coast; on a clear day you may even spot Orkney. Food served Sun–Thurs 11am–11pm, Fri–Sat 11am–1am. **££**

Dunnet Bay Caravan Club Dunnet Bay; www.caravanclub.co.uk. On the plus side is its location behind the dunes and the immaculate facilities. The bad news is that it's geared to motorhomes and is relatively expensive due to a £12 surcharge for non-Caravan Club members. March–Oct. **£**

Thurso

The town of **THURSO** may be a buzzing metropolis by the north coast's standards, but in reality it is a modest administrative service centre, most of whose visitors only pause before catching the ferry to Orkney from its port, **Scrabster**. Yet it makes a good base for exploring the area and is legendary among British **surfers**, drawn to a wave which barrels off a reef just east of the harbour. One of the most powerful waves in Europe, "Thurso East" is not a break for beginners.

The town's name derives from the Norse word *Thorsa*, literally "River of the God Thor", and in Viking times this was a major gateway to the mainland. Later, ships set sail for the Baltic and Scandinavian ports loaded with meal, beef, hides and fish. Much of the town, however, dates from the 1790s, when Sir John Sinclair built a large new extension to the old fishing port. Consequently, Thurso's grid-plan streets have some rather handsome Victorian architecture in local, greyish sandstone, not least the recently refurbished **Thurso Library**, opened in 1862 as the Miller Institute and complete with clocktower and a pillared facade. There's little sign of the town's

older roots, except for **Old St Peter's Church** up the High Street, a substantial ruin with origins in the thirteenth century. Perhaps delve more into Thurso's history at the quirky Aladdin's cave that is **Tall Tales** secondhand bookshop (1 Grove Lane).

INFORMATION AND ACTIVITIES   THURSO

Tourist information A useful website is www.discover thurso.co.uk, where you can find out about activities, events and attractions taking place in and around Thurso.

ACCOMMODATION   THURSO

Forss House Hotel 5 miles west of Thurso on A836; www.forsshousehotel.co.uk. Built in 1810 as a hunting lodge, this thirteen-bedroom hotel offers an upmarket stay, with a choice of traditional accommodation in the main house or more modern rooms in annexes. The Forss River, which wends through the grounds, offers fine salmon fishing. £££

The Marine 38 Shore St; www.themarinethurso.

co.uk. Modern furnishings and tweed headboards make for a relaxed, contemporary style. More appealing than the rooms is the small conservatory off the gorgeous breakfast room with sea views – surfers take note. ££

Sandra's Backpackers Hostel 24–26 Princes St; https://sandras-backpackers.co.uk. The only hostel in town is a clean enough, zero-frills but well-run 27-bed place. Refurbished in 2015, its small rooms are all en suite. £̄

EATING AND DRINKING

★ **Captain's Galley** Harbour, Scrabster; www.captains galley.co.uk. Fish fresh off the boat is the speciality – unfussy dishes like roast hake with borlotti broth and mussels – on three-course menus that win awards for sustainability as much as flavour. Also offers takeaway fish and chips using whichever fish is the freshest (Tues– Sat 12.30–6.30pm). Reservations essential. Easter–Oct Thurs–Sat 6.30–10pm. £̄

Thurso Community Café Thurso Harbour; 01847 892500. Home baking, toasties and home-made burgers served in a harbourside café with a laidback surf-shack vibe:

think surf-themed newspaper cuttings, colourful surfboards and driftwood art on the walls. Bring-your-own drinks on Saturday evenings during the summer (nominal corkage fee). Jan–March daily 10am–4pm; April–Dec Mon–Fri 10am–6pm, Sat 10am–8pm, Sun 10am–4pm. £̄

Y Not Bar & Grill Meadow Lane; 01847 892272. Highly rated restaurant and cocktail lounge with Sky Sports. A regularly rotating specials menu goes heavy on the fish, and there's a healthy beer selection. Also owns adjacent hotel, The Inn. Bar & Grill Sun–Thurs 8am–12am, Fri–Sat 8am–1am. £̄

West to Tongue

Vast and empty, the landscape between Thurso and Tongue has considerable drama. It's a bleak moorland intercut with sandy sea lochs and with few inhabitants: tiny **Bettyhill** is pleasant enough, as is **Tongue**, further west. But the real attraction is the landscape: as you travel west, the rich farmland of the east coast is replaced by stark heathland, with the sharp profiles of **Ben Hope** (3041ft) and **Ben Loyal** (2507ft) emerging like twin sentinels from the blanket bog of the **Flow Country** inland (see box).

Bettyhill

Thirty miles west of Thurso, **BETTYHILL** is a major crofting village, set among rocky green hills. In Gaelic it was known as *Am Blàran Odhar* ("Little Dun-coloured Field"). The origins of the English name are unknown, but it was definitely not named after Elizabeth, Countess of Sutherland, who presided over the Strathnaver Clearances and whose sorry tale is told in the town museum. The village is also surrounded on either side by beautiful beaches: **Farr beach**, a splendid crescent of white sand, is behind the Strathnaver museum, while the unbroken arc of **Torrisdale Bay** sweeps west of the town beyond the Naver River. Both receive good surf. For more cerebral pursuits, the 24-mile **Strathnaver Trail** runs south along the B873 to Altnaharra, past historical sites from the Neolithic, Bronze and Iron Age periods, as well as the remains of crofting villages cleared in the early 1800s. Free printout guides of the area are available from the museum (donations welcome).

Strathnaver Museum

In the old Farr church, east of the main village • April–Oct Mon–Sat 10am–5pm • Charge • www.strathnavermuseum.org.uk

The volunteer-run **Strathnaver Museum** houses exhibits of ethnological and archeological interest – crofting items including a bizarre fishing buoy made from a dogskin, Pictish stones and a 3800-year-old early Bronze Age beaker – and also narrates the Sutherland Clearances through a short film. Its most famous item is free to view – the **Farr stone**, a ninth-century engraved Pictish gravestone, is in the west end of the graveyard.

ACCOMMODATION AND EATING BETTYHILL

Bettyhill Hotel Main road; www.bettyhillhotel.com. A recent renovation has spruced up this 200-year-old hotel, with twenty spacious, individually furnished rooms, plus a cosy lounge. The bar hosts live, folksy music, and the on-site *Eilean Neave Restaurant* serves up Scottish dishes, like honey-roast duck breast or Scrabster scallops. Restaurant daily 6–8.30pm. **£££**

3

Tongue and around

Dominated from a hillside spur by the ruins of **Castle Varrich** (Caisteal Bharraich), a medieval stronghold of the Mackays (it's a three-mile return walk from the town centre), the pretty crofting township of **TONGUE** is strewn above the east shore of the **Kyle of Tongue**, which you can cross either via a causeway or by a longer and more scenic single-track road around its southern side. When the tide recedes, this shallow estuary becomes a mass of golden sand flats, with superb mountain views on sunny days, and the Rabbit Islands a short way out to sea. A dead-end road offers views of the islands, plus superb seascapes and scenery as it threads through Talmine towards a beach at **Strathan**; take the right turn to Melness just after the Tongue causeway.

ACCOMMODATION AND EATING TONGUE AND AROUND

Ben Loyal Tongue; https://benloyal.co.uk. Seafood fresh off the owner's boat is served in a relaxed pub with rooms, along with favourites such as steak pie or home-made burgers. With decent prices and live music most Saturdays this is the choice of many locals, while many travellers rest their weary heads upstairs – or in the glamping pods. Single rooms are especially good value. Evening meals 5–8.30pm. **£**

Kyle of Tongue Hostel & Holiday Park East of Kyle of Tongue Bridge; www.tonguehostelandholidaypark.

THE FLOW COUNTRY

East of Bettyhill, a detour inland on the A897 towards Helmsdale – turn off the coast road just before the village of Melvich – heads south into the **Flow Country** tundra. The name (pronounced to rhyme with "now") derives from *flói*, an Old Norse word meaning "marshy ground", and this 1544-square-mile expanse of "blanket bog" – the largest in the world, according to UNESCO, which is considering adding it to its World Heritage status list – is both a valuable carbon sink and home to a wide variety of birdlife. The RSPB's **Forsinard Flows Visitor Centre** (Easter–Oct daily 9am–5pm; free; www.rspb.org.uk/forsinard), at the train station in **FORSINARD**, is the gateway to the so-called Forsinard Flows. Pick up a leaflet on the mile-long **Dubh Lochan Trail**, then follow the boardwalk to the Flows Lookout Tower before walking over flagstones to learn about its blanket bog. En route, you get to see bog asphodel, bogbean, and insect-trapping sundew and butterwort; you've also got a good chance of spotting greenshanks, golden plovers and hen harriers. In summer, the visitor centre runs **guided walks** through the area to explain the wonders of peat; wellies or walking boots are recommended.

NORTH-COAST WALKING AND CYCLING

Ordnance Survey Explorer maps 447 & 448

Rising up from the southern end of the Kyle of Tongue, Ben Hope and Ben Loyal offer moderate-to-hard walks, rewarded on a decent day by vast views over the empty landscape. **Ben Hope** (3041ft), which was given its name ("Hill of the Bay") by the Vikings, is the most northerly of Scotland's Munros – they say that from its summit at the summer equinox, the sun never vanishes entirely beneath the horizon. It's surprisingly accessible – the best approach is a four-hour round trip from the road that runs down the west side of Loch Hope. Start at a sheep shed by the roadside, just under two miles beyond the southern end of Loch Hope.

Ben Loyal (2507ft), though lower, is a longer hike at around six hours. To avoid the worst of the bogs, follow the northern spur from Ribigill Farm, a mile south of Tongue. At the end of the southbound farm-track, a path emerges; follow this up a steepish slope to gain the first peak on the ridge from where the walking to the top is easier.

For **shorter walks** or **cycles**, there are well-marked woodland trails at **Borgie Forest**, six miles east of Tongue, and **Truderscraig Forest** by Syre, twelve miles south of Bettyhill on the B871. Near the entrance to Borgie Forest is the *a'chraobh*, a spiral feature created using native trees and carved local stone. If you follow the signs to "**Rosal Pre-Clearance Village**", a stop on the Strathnaver Trail (see above), you'll find an area clear of trees with what little remains of the village – fifteen families were evicted between 1814 and 1818. Information boards explain the crofters' lifestyles in the eighteenth century before the upheavals of the Highland Clearances.

co.uk. The Duke of Sutherland's old shooting lodge has been repurposed as a large, well-equipped hostel with spacious dorms and family rooms, plus great mountain views. It's SYHA-affiliated too. **Mid-April to Sept.** £̄

★ **Tongue Hotel** Tongue; www.tonguehotel.co.uk. This nineteen-bedroom small hotel marries a relaxed modern vibe with the architectural heritage of a former ducal hunting lodge. Highland Coast Hotels acquired the property in 2022 and completed a much-needed renovation, enhancing its earthy tones and sprucing up its bar, restaurant and feature suite to be even more inviting. **£££**

A WALKER CLIMBING THE ASCENT UP TO STAC POLLAIDH

Exploring the northwest

The far northwest Highlands capture the stark, elemental beauty of the country like nowhere else. Here, as the geology shifts into ice-scoured pinkish quartzite barely covered by a thin skin of moorland, peaks become more widely spaced and settlements smaller and fewer, linked by twisting roads and shoreside footpaths. On the road from Durness to Ullapool, life feels exhilaratingly on the edge of civilization. The flip side is that accommodation and food are sparse; be prepared that places get booked up fast in season and the options are thin on the ground during winter.

HIGHLIGHTS

❶ **Sandwood Bay** Set off for a four-mile walk to the remote and wind-lashed Sandwood Bay, one of the most beautiful beaches in Scotland; keep going for the intrepid, full-day trek to Cape Wrath. See page 63

❷ **Handa Island** The wildlife reserve of Handa Island is cloaked with machair and purple heather, and home to one of the largest seabird colonies in northwest Europe – razorbills, guillemots and puffins in their thousands. See page 63

❸ **Foodie Lochinver** The Highlands' foodie capital offers everything from slap-up pies to sophisticated cuisine, with some Scottish tapas thrown in for good measure. See page 67

❹ **Walks in Assynt** Take your pick from the sugarloaf peaks that pepper the Assynt landscape. The scramble to the top of Stac Pollaidh rewards with panoramic views, while the iconic Suilven offers a trickier eight-mile ascent. See page 64

❺ **Ullapool** A metropolis in these parts, Ullapool has a number of atmospheric drinking holes and quality restaurants to warm up windswept cheeks; if you're lucky, you may stumble across some live music. See page 69

If there's one part of the North Coast 500 to take slow, it's the Durness to Ullapool leg. Truly adventurous sorts shouldn't think twice about a hike to **Cape Wrath**, or at the very least they should embark on the eight-mile round walk to the wonderful **Sandwood Bay**. Heading south, **Scourie** offers some of the best fly-fishing opportunities in the Highlands, while **Assynt** and **Coigach** have a string of epic summits to bag – Suilven being the king of the bunch. The hair-raising B869 via Drumbeg is at once thrilling and stomach-churning, wrapping around the coast to foodie **Lochinver**, which has the most concentrated and finest selection of fine-dining options along the entire North Coast 500. In **Ullapool**, the most built-up settlement hereabouts, the riotous pubs and sleepy waterfront setting make it a compulsory pit stop before the journey south into Wester Ross.

GETTING AROUND

Heading south of Durness into the northwest Highlands, **drivers** will face the most challenging and breathtaking section of the entire North Coast 500. The A838 is mostly single-track from Durness to Rhiconich, where it widens, turns into the A894 and hugs the coast down to Kylesku and its photogenic curving bridge. Shortly afterwards, the route takes a right turn onto the B869. This winding, up-and-down road is not suitable for **larger vehicles**, like caravans or camper vans, nor for inexperienced or unconfident drivers. To bypass it, drivers can stick to the A894 and either turn right on the A837 to Lochinver, or carry on south to Ullapool. **Cyclists** face a truly rewarding cycle, with some of the best climbs and downhills in the Highlands; there's a steep ascent just south of Durness, and another tough climb south of Unapool, with a cracking downhill to look forward to shortly after the Knockan Crag National Reserve. Pedallers should be prepared that the 24-mile B869 coastal route to Lochinver has a total elevation of over 2000ft.

Durness and around

Scattered over sheltered sandy coves and grassy clifftops, **DURNESS** is the most northwesterly village on the British mainland, straddling the point where the road swings from the fertile limestone machair of the north coast to the undulating quartzite landscape of the northwest. The village sits above Sango Sands bay, whose fine beach has made it a modest resort. Beatle **John Lennon** came here as a teenager on family holidays to stay with his Auntie Lizzie (Elizabeth Parkes) – his memories later went into the song *In My Life*, and he revisited in 1969 with Yoko. Parkes is buried in the graveyard at Balnakeil, and there is a slightly bizarre memorial to Lennon at the Durness Village Hall which still attracts a trickle of die-hard Beatles fans.

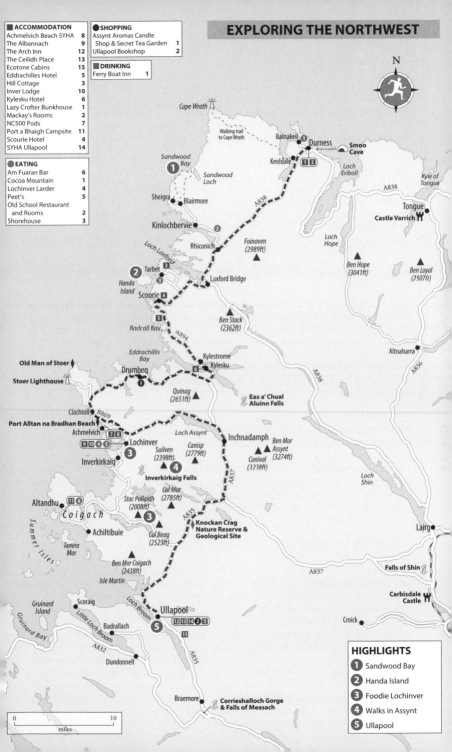

EXPLORING THE NORTHWEST

N

Cape Wrath

Walking trail
to Cape Wrath

Sandwood
Bay

Balnakeil
Durness
Smoo
Cave
Keoldale
Loch
Eriboll
Kyle of
Tongue

Sandwood
Loch

A838

Tongue
Castle Varrich

Sheigra
Blairmore

Kinlochbervie

Loch Laxford

Rhiconich

Foinaven
(2989ft)

Loch
Hope

Ben Hope
(3041ft)

Ben Loyal
(2507ft)

Tarbet

Handa
Island

Laxford Bridge

Scourie

Ben Stack
(2362ft)

Altnaharra

Badcall Bay

A894

Eddrachillis
Bay

Kylestrome
Kylesku

A838

A836

Old Man of Stoer

Stoer Lighthouse

Drumbeg

Quinag
(2651ft)

Eas a' Chual
Aluinn Falls

Clachtoll

B869

Port Alltan na Bradhan Beach

Achmelvich

Lochinver

Loch Assynt

Inchnadamph

Ben Mor
Assynt
(3274ft)

Conival
(3238ft)

A837

Loch
Shin

Inverkirkaig

Suilven
(2398ft)

Canisp
(2779ft)

Inverkirkaig Falls

Cul Mor
(2785ft)

Lairg

Altandhu

Coigach

Stac Pollaidh
(2008ft)

Cul Beag
(2523ft)

A835

Knockan Crag
Nature Reserve &
Geological Site

Achiltibuie

Falls of Shin

Ben Mor Coigach
(2438ft)

A837

Carbisdale
Castle

Isle Martin

Tanera
Mor

Summer Isles

Gruinard
Island

Scoraig

Badrallach

Loch Broom

Ullapool

Croick

Little Loch Broom

A832

Dundonnell

A835

Gruinard Bay

Braemore

Corrieshalloch Gorge
& Falls of Measach

0   10
miles

HIGHLIGHTS

1 Sandwood Bay
2 Handa Island
3 Foodie Lochinver
4 Walks in Assynt
5 Ullapool

Smoo Cave

1 mile east of Durness • Always open • Free; charge for dinghy tours

A mile east of the village is **Smoo Cave**, a gaping hole in a limestone cliff created by the sea and a small burn. Tucked at the end of a narrow sea cove, the main chamber is accessible via steps from the car park. The much-hyped rock formations are quite impressive, and if the weather behaves you can take a fantastic twenty-minute trip by rubber dinghy (run on demand Easter–Oct; www.smoocavetours.com) into two further caverns; after heavy rain a waterfall cascades through the middle of the cavern.

Balnakeil

A mile northwest of Durness, the white sands of **Balnakeil Bay** are stunning in any weather, but especially spectacular when sunny days turn the sea a brilliant Mediterranean turquoise. A path winds north through the dunes behind to reach **Faraid Head** – fine views east to the mouth of Loch Eriboll and west to Cape Wrath make this circuit (3–4hr) the best in the area. While here, drop by the **Balnakeil Craft Village**, a hippie commune born out of a disused 1970s military camp.

Cape Wrath

Closer to Iceland than to London, the headland takes its name not from stormy seas but from the Norse word *hvarf* ("turning place"), a throwback to the days when Viking warships passed en route to raid the Scottish coast. Yet **Cape Wrath** still exudes a powerful sense of nature in the raw. The British mainland's most northwesterly point – and one of only two capes in the country – is tipped by a Stevenson lighthouse and stands above **Clo Mor cliffs**, the highest sea cliffs in Britain and a prime breeding site for seabirds. On a clear day you can see as far as Orkney and the Outer Hebrides.

INFORMATION AND ACTIVITIES   DURNESS AND AROUND

Tourist information A useful website for Durness is www.durness.org; information on Cape Wrath can be found at www.visitcapewrath.com.

Durness golf course Durness; www.durnessgolfclub.org. The most northwesterly course on mainland Britain is a nine-hole with two tee-off options per hole to create 18 holes. Rent equipment from the clubhouse. Closed to visitors Sun morning.

Golden Eagle Zipline 3.5 miles east of Durness; www.durnesszipline.com. You'll pass Britain's most northerly zipline before arriving in Durness so add this to your plans if you fancy zipping 45mph above the pink-hued sands of Ceannabeinne Beach. £15pp. No bookings due to weather dependency, just turn up; Easter–Aug 10.15am–5pm, Sept–Oct 10.30am–3.30pm.

ACCOMMODATION AND EATING

DURNESS

Lazy Crofter Bunkhouse www.visitdurness.com/bunk house. Run year-round by *Mackay's* next door, this is the finest bunkhouse on the north coast, far more appealing than the SYHA hostel by Smoo Cave. Has a snug cabin atmosphere and gets extra marks for individual reading lights in compact twins and two dorms. The terrace has sea views. Sleeps twenty. Easter–Oct. £

★ **Mackay's Rooms** www.visitdurness.com/rooms. Handmade and vintage furniture, luxury linen, natural colours and genuine hospitality make this one of the best stays on the north coast. It also manages weekly self-catering options: from a sweet cabin to carbon-negative

Croft 103's eco-chic. No dinners, but they compensate for it with superb breakfasts, picnic lunches and afternoon tea, plus nibbles in the evenings. May–Oct. ££

BALNAKEIL

Cocoa Mountain Balnakeil Craft Village; www.cocoa mountain.co.uk. "The Best Hot Chocolate", a rich bitter-sweet hot chocolate topped off by white chocolate, is the speciality in the bright modern café of this chocolatier. Sells snacks plus its own chocolates and truffles. A treat after time in the wilds. Call out of season and the friendly owner may open up for you. Easter–Oct Mon–Sat 9am–5pm. £

South to Scourie

The road heading south from Durness to Scourie sweeps through the Highlands at their starkest – rocks piled on rocks, bog and water, and a bare, stony coastline that looks increasingly inhospitable. For some that's a call to adventure: sailor and explorer John Ridgway established an outdoor school on an isolated sea loch off **Loch Laxford** in the 1960s.

Kinlochbervie

The largest settlement here, reached on the B801, is **KINLOCHBERVIE**, where a huge fish market and harbour reveal this as the premier fishing port in the area, reduced in stature since its heyday in the late 1980s, but still serviced by trucks from all over Europe. Otherwise it's a scruffy, utilitarian place, usually visited only as a launchpad for Sandwood Bay (see below).

ACCOMMODATION AND EATING — KINLOCHBERVIE

Old School Restaurant and Rooms Inshegra, 1 mile before Kinlochbervie on B801; www.oldschoolhotel. co.uk. By far the most comfortable accommodation option in the area, with a handful of rather smart rooms, including a cute separate en-suite single. Guests are treated to good-value evening meals of home-cooking: expect haddock chowder, venison casserole or veggie lasagne. March–October. **££**

Sandwood Bay

A single-track road continues northwest of Kinlochbervie through **OLDSHOREMORE**, an isolated crofters' village above a stunning white-sand beach (a magic spot to wild camp), then on to **BLAIRMORE**, start of the four-mile walk to **Sandwood Bay**. The shell-white **beach** beyond the peat moors is one of the most beautiful in Scotland, flanked by rolling dunes and lashed by gales for much of the year. Vikings beached their longships here over a millennium ago – the name is a corruption of "sand" and "vatn", meaning sand and water. Good luck with them both if you decide to wild camp here. It's possible to trek overland from Sandwood Bay north to Cape Wrath (see page 62), the northwestern tip of mainland Britain, a full day's walk away.

4

Scourie and around

Twenty five miles south of Durness, **SCOURIE** lies among a landscape marbled with lochs and lochans. This is prime Scottish **fly-fishing** territory; permits are available for a small fee from the Fishing Tackle Shop in the garage (http://scouriefillingstation. uk). There's also some terrific **walking** hereabouts, up mountains like Ben Stack (2362ft) – locals yarn that its pyramidal peak inspired a visiting Hollywood executive to create the logo for Paramount Pictures – and a beautiful beach makes it a good choice for families.

Handa Island

Managed by the Scottish Wildlife Trust (www.scottishwildlifetrust.org.uk) • No charge to visit, but donations welcomed • Ferries run April–Sept Mon–Sat 9am–2pm, every 20–30min • Charge

Reason enough to come through Scourie is **Handa Island**, a huge chunk of red Torridon sandstone just offshore. Carpeted with machair and purple heather, the island is maintained as a **wildlife reserve** by the Scottish Wildlife Trust and supports one of the largest seabird colonies in northwest Europe – razorbills and Britain's largest breeding colony of guillemots gather on ragged sandstone cliffs in summer, while puffins nest in clifftop burrows from late May to mid-July.

Ferries shuttle regularly in summer from **Tarbet**, a six-mile drive north of Scourie. When you arrive on Handa Island you will be greeted by a volunteer, who offers an introductory talk on the history and ecology of the island. Allow three hours at least to follow a **footpath** around the island – an easy and enjoyable walk taking in Great Stack, a 361ft rock pillar on the north shore, and fine views across the Minch.

ACCOMMODATION AND EATING   SCOURIE AND AROUND

Eddrachilles Hotel On the A894, 2 miles south of Scourie; www.eddrachilles.com. This eighteenth-century former manse is all about the views; the sunsets over Badcall Bay are unbeatable. Basic rooms offer a pleasant stay while the dining room, with impressive flagstone floors, serves up fine food, including shellfish caught in the bay. April–Oct. **££££**

Hill Cottage Fanagmore, 3 miles off the A894, 1 mile north of Tarbet; https://hillcottagesutherland.com. This old crofting house offers the ultimate escape from civilization. The no-frills decor makes for a comfortable if nostalgic stay, with its electric fireplace and floral furnishings. But a decent DVD collection and – remarkably – fast wi-fi connect guests to the twenty-first century. The conservatory has a rocking chair and wonderful views out to Loch Laxford. March–Nov, weekly bookings. **££**

Scourie Hotel Scourie; https://scouriehotel.com. A

traditional, family-run coaching inn whose fishing obsession only adds character. There are taxidermied trout in the wood-panelled cocktail bar, real ales in the public bar and enormous maps of Scotland in the entrance hall. Themed Highlands headboards are a nice touch in the simple, elegant rooms. There's a seasonal – and reasonably priced – four-course dining menu, or less expensive bar meals like fish and chips. A memorable stay. April–Sept. **£££**

★ **Shorehouse** Tarbet wharf; http://shorehouse tarbet.co.uk. With its views of pristine shore, Handa and the Old Man of Stoer beyond, this feels like the restaurant at the end of the world. Nautical and airy inside, serving home-made soups and sandwiches, plus mains of salmon, hot mackerel and seafood platters. The food on your plate couldn't be much fresher – they catch their own shellfish. April–Sept Mon–Sat noon–7pm, until 8pm July & Aug. **££**

Assynt

The **Assynt** region has an epic, almost cinematic, quality. Marking the transition from Sutherland into Wester Ross, this region is one of the least populated areas in Europe and its landscape consists not of mountain ranges but of extraordinary peaks which rise individually from the moorland. See a mountain like **Suilven** and you understand why the name is said to derive from "A-ssynt", meaning seen from afar, or "ass" – the Old Norse word for rocky. Certainly, Assynt boasts some of the world's oldest rock formations, and roadside signs highlight the region's geological importance as the **Northwest Highlands Geopark** (www.nwhgeopark.com).

This is splendid touring country: an area of peaceful backroads which twist past crofts to deserted beaches or headlands with superb views to the Outer Hebrides. **Lochinver**, the main settlement, makes a fine base – it has peaks like Suilven within reach and is also acquiring a foodie reputation. There are appealing crofting villages to discover around **Achiltibuie** and two Munros to bag above **Inchnadamph**, where there's also a three-mile walk through a limestone valley to the dramatic **Bone Caves**.

Kylesku

Until a road bridge swept over the mouth of lochs Glencoul and Glendhu, **KYLESKU**, 33 miles north of Ullapool, was the embarkation point for a ferry that was the only link from the west Highlands to north Scotland. Off the main road since the bridge's construction in 1984, it's now a beautiful, soporific spot, where interlocking slopes plunge into the deep waters. Marking a last hurrah before the Assynt's sharp sandstone gives way to rounded quartzite, Kylesku is popular with walkers due to its proximity to **Quinag** (2651ft), less than a single peak than several peaks reached by a **ridge walk**. The easiest ascent is from a car park on the A894 a few miles south of Kylesku. Also

in the area is Britain's highest waterfall, **Eas a' Chual Aluinn** (650ft), at the head of Loch Glencoul. It's a five-mile return walk that heads east from a car park two miles south of Kylesku, or a full-day walk on a track around the north side of both lochs. Alternatively, boat tours run from the wharf in Kylesku.

INFORMATION AND ACTIVITIES   KYLESKU

Tourist office The North West Highlands Geopark visitor centre and café, *The Rock Stop* (Sun–Fri 10am–5pm, Sat 9am–5pm, www.nwhgeopark.com), is based in Kylesku's old Unapool School Building. It has information on the region, plus hot drinks and sandwiches.

Northwest Sea Tours Kylesku; https://northwest seatours.co.uk. Gentle cruises into lochs Glendhu and Glencoul (3 daily, round trip 1hr 15min, from £22). April–Sept.

ACCOMMODATION AND EATING

Kylesku Hotel Kylesku; www.kyleskuhotel.co.uk. A small hotel in a crisp, modern style beside the loch. It provides by far the best food in the area, all sourced locally – from the vegetables to the shellfish. Expect the likes of Kylesku langoustines or hogget curry. The smart "Willy's Hoose" wing is named after a local – some rooms have a private balcony and loch views. Feb–Nov. **££££**

South to Lochinver

There are two routes from Kylesku to Lochinver: continue south on the A894 then turn right onto the fast A837 along the shore of Loch Assynt (see below), or take the scenic B869 coast road. Hugging the indented shoreline, the latter offers coastal views,

4

WALKS IN COIGACH AND ASSYNT

Ordnance Survey Explorer map 442

Of Coigach's and Assynt's spectacular array of idiosyncratic peaks, **Stac Pollaidh** (2008ft) counts as the most accessible and popular hike – so much so that the path is often repaired and re-routed up the mountain from a car park on the Achiltibuie road. It now leads walkers around the northern side of the hill before climbing steeply. You'll need a head for heights on the jagged summit ridge – turn back from the summit if you feel uncertain about basic rock-climbing.

Suilven (2398ft) is the most memorable of the Assynt peaks – "one sandstone chord that holds up time in space", said poet Norman McCaig of its weird sugar-loaf profile. The ascent is a tough eight-hour trip that starts with a boggy five-mile walk to the base. From the A837 at Elphin, head around the north of Cam Loch then through the glen between Canisp and Suilven, to pick up a path that aims for the saddle – Bealach Mor – in the middle of Suilven's summit ridge, from where the path to the top is straightforward. The return is by the same route, although at the saddle you could choose to turn southwest for the route to Inverkirkaig.

The highest peaks in Assynt are **Conival** (3238ft) and **Ben Mor Assynt** (3274ft), often climbed as Munros even though they're less distinctive than their neighbours, and are known for their bleak landscapes. The route follows the track up Glen Dubh from Inchnadamph; stay to the north of the river and aim for the saddle between Conival and the peak to the north, Beinn an Fhurain. On the ridge, turn southeast to climb to the summit of Conival then east along a high ridge to the top of Ben Mor. The entire walk, including the return to Inchnadamph, takes five to six hours.

For something less testing there are some classic **coastal walks** immediately north of Lochinver. From **Baddidarrach**, a path with fantastic views of the Assynt peaks leads over heather slopes to Loch Dubh and down to **Achmelvich** (1hr). From here there's a sporadically signposted but reasonable path to **Clachtoll** (about 2hr) past delightful sandy coves, grassy knolls, old watermills and rocks at low tide. More dramatic still is the ninety-minute clifftop circuit from Stoer lighthouse to the famous stack, **The Old Man of Stoer**.

superb **beaches** and high cliff walks. The first village worth a stopping at is **DRUMBEG**, before continuing round to the beautiful strand at **CLACHTOLL**. The tiny, hidden **Port Alltan na Bradhan** cove lies a couple of miles beyond. At **ACHMELVICH**, four miles before reaching Lochinver, a tiny bay cradles a white-sand beach lapped by azure water.

Old Man of Stoer

A side road that branches north off the B869 between **STOER** and **CLASHNESSIE** ends abruptly by a lighthouse near **Raffin**. The reason to come is a two-mile stroll along a boggy track to reach the **Old Man of Stoer**, a 197ft rock stack just off the Point of Stoer, the headland's tip, surrounded by sheer cliffs and occasionally scaled by climbers. It's worth a circuit around the south side of the headland to return with a vast view of the mountains of Assynt, after which you'll deserve a cuppa in the tea van at the car park (April–Sept Mon–Fri & Sun 11am–5pm, except in high winds and heavy rain).

ACCOMMODATION AND EATING   **SOUTH TO LOCHINVER**

Achmelvich Beach SYHA Achmelvich; www.hostelling scotland.org.uk. Although the open-plan lounge-kitchen of this 22-bed hostel in a former school and cottage struggles when full, most people are outside anyway — just 100yds away are the white sands of the beach. Dorms, a family room and private twins are available. Closed mid-Sept to Easter, as well as weekdays Sept & Easter; whole hostel rental available all year. £

NC500 Pods Achmelvich Bay; https://nc500pods.co.uk. Arguably the most famous glamping pods on the entire North Coast 500, and with views across Achmelvich Bay you can see why. Pods include kitchen facilities and private bathrooms; they're very well designed given the space limitations. Considerably cheaper out of high-season. ££££

SHOPPING

Assynt Aromas Candle Shop & Secret Tea Garden Drumbeg; www.assyntaromas.co.uk. An essential stop-off for anyone travelling along the wiggling coastal route to Lochinver. The aromatic candles and soaps on sale are lovingly handmade on-site, and can only be bought here. Through the back of the shop, the *Secret Garden* offers a tranquil spot to have a cup of tea (including peppermint, for anyone suffering from car sickness) with some cake. June–Aug daily 10.30am–5pm (tearoom till 4.30pm); April, May, Sept & Oct closed Mon.

4

Loch Assynt and around

Bounded by peaks of the Ben Mor Assynt massif, the area inland from Lochinver is a wilderness of mountains, moorland, mist and scree. Anglers love it because of the brown trout in its lochs and lochans, while the toothy remains of **Ardveck Castle**, a MacLeod stronghold from 1597 that fell to the Seaforth Mackenzies after a siege in 1691, add romance. The region's other claim to fame is **Knockan Crag** (Creag a' Chnocain; www.nature.scot/enjoying-outdoors), eleven miles south of Loch Assynt on the A835 to Ullapool, one of the world's most important geological sites. In 1859 geologist James Nicol came up with the theory of thrust faults from its geology. Two interpretive **trails** (15min and 1hr) highlight the movement of rock plates for novices and there's information on the area in an unstaffed **visitor centre**.

Lochinver and around

The small town (oversized village, really) of **LOCHINVER** is one of the busier fishing harbours in Scotland, and has a pleasingly down-to-earth atmosphere. Factor in excellent accommodation, both budget and high-end, and an established reputation for food, and it makes a natural base for the area.

It's hard to think of a more beautiful route than the single-track road that wriggles south from Lochinver towards Coigach, via Inverkirkaig, the start of two fantastic walks (see box). Unremittingly spectacular, the journey is the Highlands in miniature, threading through stunted beech woods, heaving valleys, open moorland and bare rock, past the distinct sugar-loaf **Suilven** (2398ft) and the startling shapes of Cul Beag (2523ft) and Cul Mor (2785ft).

Inverkirkaig Falls and Suilven

A car park at the south end of Inverkirkaig, three miles south of Lochinver, marks the start of a **walk** upriver to **Falls of Kirkaig**, itself the start of a long but gentle walk to the base of **Suilven** – its huge sandstone dome is as much of a landmark today as it was for Viking sailors. Serious hikers use the path as an approach to scale the peak (10–12hr), but you can also follow it for an easy five-mile, three-hour (return) ramble, taking in a waterfall and a secluded loch.

ACCOMMODATION AND EATING   **LOCHINVER AND AROUND**

Some of the local accommodation is in a conjoined village, **Baddidarrach**, on the north side of the loch; from Lochinver, cross the bridge and turn left.

The Albannach Baddidarrach; https://thealbannach. co.uk. Lesley Crosfield and Colin Craig's Victorian house provides a stay of exquisite taste and astonishing views over the walled garden to the sea loch and Suilven beyond. Individually decorated rooms vary from romantic to hip, with great bathrooms. Two-night minimum stay, and no children under 12. Food served from 6pm: Feb–March Fri–Sun, April–Nov & late Dec Tues–Sun. **£££**

Peet's Culag Road, Lochinver; https://peets.co.uk. Peet's is a family-run harbourside eatery, serving delicious food from locally sourced produce. Menus are seasonal and naturally feature a lot of fantastically fresh seafood alongside high-quality staples like burgers and steak – but there is a great selection of vegan options as well. You can expect a friendly welcome and spectacular views across the clear waters of the loch. Sun–Fri 5.30–7.30pm. **££**

Inver Lodge Signed off Main St, Lochinver; www. inverlodge.com. This refurbished hillside hotel makes for a five-star stay, featuring relaxed contemporary decor with a nod to Highlands country style and loch views. The latter are at their best from the Inver Lodge restaurant, with fresh seafood plus steaks and game. April–Oct daily 6–9pm. **£££**

★ **Lochinver Larder** Main St, near bridge; www. lochinverlarder.com. Sensational home-made pies, featuring exotic ingredients like wild boar and saag paneer, have made it famous, but this fine bistro prepares other food too: think smoked fish linguini, home-made fishcakes, or langoustine in lime, ginger and chilli butter. Takeaway available. Mon–Sat 9am–4pm. **£**

Coigach

Coigach is the peninsula immediately south of Lochinver, accessible via a road signposted to Achiltibuie off the A835. It's a beautiful drive, squeezing between the northern shore of Loch Lurgainn and mountains like mammoths, including **Cul Beag** (2523ft), craggy **Stac Pollaidh** (2008ft) and the awesome bulk of **Ben Mor Coigach** (2438ft), southeast, which presides over the area. There's some spectacular coastal scenery too. It's a place to unwind, with gorgeous views of the Summer Isles scattered offshore and signposted trails along coastal moors and mountains. If the steep Ben Mor Coigach–Sgurr an Fhidhleir horseshoe (7 miles; 7hr) seems too tough, the Culnacraig circuit (5 miles; 2hr) between Achduart and Culnacraig offers great views. Coigach's main settlement is **ACHILTIBUIE**, a crofting village spread above beaches and rocks, and offering astonishing sunsets.

Tanera Mor

A mile offshore, **Tanera Mor** is the largest island of the **Summer Isles**. It briefly hit the headlines in March 2016 when its family custodians put it up for sale after a community buyout failed. In 2017, the island was purchased by a wealthy British businessman for £1.7 million. At the time of writing, the island was undergoing a major restoration project intended to transform Tanera Mor into an idyllic retreat (https://summer-isles.com). In the meantime, **boat** trips from Old Dorney Harbour, just north of Achiltibuie (Shearwater Cruises, www.summerqueen.co.uk) round the isles to put ashore on Tanera Mor are still possible, allowing visitors to potter up to the post office to buy "Summer Isles" stamps or have a cuppa in a small café by the pier.

INFORMATION AND ACTIVITIES	COIGACH

Tourist information Useful websites include https:// visitcoigach.com, or https://summer-isles.com for Tanera Mor.

Hamlet Mountaineering Achiltibuie; www.hamlet mountaineering.com. This highly professional outfit,

run by mountaineering expert and local mountain rescue worker, Tim Hamlet, offers outdoor excursions in Assynt. Trips include everything from scrambling to sea-kayaking and rock climbing – whatever the weather. Custom day rates apply; contact for prices.

ACCOMMODATION AND EATING

Am Fuaran Bar Altandhu; www.amfuaran.co.uk. A lovely pub whatever the exterior suggests, as cosy as a cabin inside – log-burner and all – and with a fine menu of steak-and-ale pies, chickpea tagine and a selection of Ross-Shire steaks. Mon–Thurs 11am–11.45pm, Fri noon–11.45pm, Sat noon–midnight, Sun 12.30–11pm. **£££**

Port A Bhaigh Campsite Althandhu; https://porta bhaigh.co.uk. Spread behind the beach with mesmerizing sea views to the Summer Isles and excellent facilities that include a laundry, this is as fine a campsite as you'll find in the Highlands. Midges can be horrendous but the *Am Fuaran Bar* is literally over the road. **£**

Ullapool

ULLAPOOL, the northwest's principal town, is an appealing place spread across a sheltered arm of land in Loch Broom – a perfect base for exploring the northwest Highlands. Here you'll find all the cultural life of the only town worth the title in the region, with a penchant for barnstorming live music nights and a few excellent restaurants. Founded by the British Fisheries Society at the height of the herring boom in 1788, the grid-plan town remains an important fishing centre, which gives it a salty authenticity despite the hundreds of visitors who pass through in high season, bound north or to catch the **ferry** to Stornoway on Lewis.

4

Ullapool Museum

7–8 West Argyle St • Easter–Oct Mon–Fri 10am–5pm, Sat 10am–4pm • Charge • www.ullapoolmuseum.co.uk

The only conventional attraction in town, the community-run **Ullapool Museum**, in the old parish church, uses photographs and audio-visual displays to provide an insight into crofting, fishing, local weather and emigration. During the Clearances, Ullapool was one of the ports through which evicted crofters left to start new lives abroad – it also has some genealogy resources.

Isle Martin

www.islemartin.org

Three miles northwest of Ullapool in Loch Broom, **Isle Martin** was inhabited on and off for a few thousand years – they say it was named after a follower of St Colomba, who may be under a fifth-century gravestone in the old graveyard – until the last crofting families called it a day in 1949. Gifted to the RSPB in 1999, the four-hundred-acre island is a romantic spot to be a temporary castaway, with beaches, walks and views to the cliffs of Ben Mor Coigach and the Summer Isles. Bothy-style accommodation is available in the *Croft House* or bunk rooms in the *Mill House*. At the time of research no scheduled ferries were running to the island, but the local community has recently bought a boat named "Auk," which serves as a seasonal passenger ferry and work boat alike. Visitors can also get over on a fishing boat with advance notice (contact Ullapool's tourist office; see below), or via a RIB trip with Seascape Expeditions.

Summer Isles

During summer, the *Summer Queen* steamer (May to early Sept Mon–Sat; www. summerqueen.co.uk) and the RIB-safari operator Seascape Expeditions (Easter–Sept, depending on weather; www.sea-scape.co.uk), run wildlife cruises and trips to the **Summer Isles**, twelve miles west of Ullapool, to view seabird colonies, grey seals, dolphins, porpoises and the occasional whale. Whether slow and stately or fast and full-on in caves, it's a trip worth taking (weather permitting).

INFORMATION AND ACTIVITIES ULLAPOOL

Tourist office Argyle St (Mon–Sat, 9am–5pm) This friendly, well-run tourist iCentre also offers an accommodation booking service (www.visitscotland.com); www.ullapool.com is also a handy resource.

★ **McKenzie Mountaineering** Ullapool; www. mckenziemountaineering.com. Year-round guided walking adventures around the west coast and beyond, from their base in Ullapool. Ben and Rosie's love for the local area is clear to see; a hike up Ullapool Hill (846ft) is a great start, but enquire about multi-day walks too. 1-day trips from £40pp.

Seascape Expeditions Ullapool; www.sea-scape. co.uk. RIB-safari operator offers high-octane wildlife cruises to the Summer Isles and Loch Broom, plus private trips. Weather-dependent. From £27.50pp. Easter–Sept.

Shearwater Cruises Ullapool; www.summerqueen. co.uk. Wildlife cruises and trips to the Summer Isles (see opposite), twelve miles west of Ullapool, to view seabird colonies, grey seals, dolphins, porpoises and the occasional whale. From £40pp. May to early Sept Mon–Sat.

ACCOMMODATION AND EATING

Ullapool is busy from Easter through until September – **booking in advance** is essential.

The Arch Inn West Shore St; www.thearchinn.co.uk. Ullapool's liveliest pub divides between a popular bar and informal restaurant with Scottish-European cooking: starters like sautéed scallops with pickled apple, plus sirloin steak alongside the usual fish and chips. The sophisticated, unfussy rooms have lovely views over Loch Broom and are fitted with modern bathrooms. Mon–Thurs noon–10pm, Fri–Sun noon–11pm; food served Easter–Oct. **££**

The Ceilidh Place West Argyle St; www.theceilidh place.com. Antique bed frames, old books on vintage cabinets and Roberts radios add character to the rooms of this lovely small hotel, where the mantra is "no TVs, and proud". Some rooms are pepped up with stylish wallpaper, otherwise modern-rustic rules: the cheapest rooms share bathrooms. It also manages a bunkhouse directly opposite. The lounge and library, with honesty bar, offers sophisticated relaxation, while the bistro menu downstairs features home-made burgers, salads, schnitzels, plus good

value daily specials like risotto and fish casseroles – and its bar hosts regular live music. **££**

★ **Ecotone Cabins** 3 miles south of Ullapool, just off the A835; www.ecotonecabins.com. Seriously cosy eco-friendly, self-catered cabins where regenerative tourism is the aim. Kitchens are kitted out with every appliance you could need; there's plenty of wardrobe space too. Owned and operated by the Planterose family who own the surrounding Leckmelm forest – profits directly support projects to regenerate the land and benefit the local community. Welcome pack of eggs and vegetables from their allotment, plus locally sourced chocolate and strawberry jam a nice touch. **££**

SYHA Ullapool Shore St; www.hostellingscotland. org.uk. Busy hostel bang on the seafront, where prints and murals of seaside scenes help add a cheerful holiday atmosphere. There are dorms of various sizes, doubles, twins, two lounges, internet access and laundry plus lots of good information about local walks. April–Oct. **£**

DRINKING

Ullapool has no shortage of decent boozers. The liveliest pub around, the *Arch Inn*, hosts live bands while you can often hear live Scottish **folk music** at *The Ceilidh Place* (see above).

Ferry Boat Inn Shore St; www.fbiullapool.com. Popular with locals, the *FBI* is a fine spot to swig a pint of ale at the lochside (midges permitting) and watch the boats. It hosts live music, and also at its sister pub *The Argyll* round the corner. Daily 11am–11pm. **£**

SHOPPING

Ullapool Bookshop Quay St; www.ullapoolbookshop. co.uk. Cute bookstore near the harbour stocking new novels, Scottish history, maps and guides. If there was

one bookshop to visit on the west coast, this would be it. Keep an eye out for local author book signings. Mon–Sat 9am–5pm, Sun 11am–5pm.

VIEW OF THE ISLE OF SKYE FROM REDPOINT BEACH

Wester Ross to Inverness

All the classic elements of Scotland's coastal scenery – craggy mountains, sandy beaches, whitewashed crofting cottages and shimmering island views – come together in Wester Ross. Settlements such as Applecross and the peninsulas north and south of Gairloch maintain a simplicity and sense of isolation outside of peak season. There is some tough but wonderful hiking in the mountains around Torridon, while boat trips and the prolific marine life and birdlife draw nature-lovers. Anyone with green fingers will enjoy this part of the route, too, as there are two excellent botanical gardens – Inverewe and Attadale – each with spectacular plants from around the world.

5

HIGHLIGHTS

❶ **Aultbea** This unsung wee hamlet has a lovely perfume studio with a café and canoeing trips on offer which make it a hidden delight on the North Coast 500. See page 74

❷ **Subtropical gardens** The riotously colourful Inverewe and Attadale gardens have plants from all around the world; a slice of the tropics in the unlikeliest corner of Britain. See page 74 and 80

❸ **Marine life in Gairloch** This is one of the top places along the North Coast 500 for a

marine wildlife safari; minke whales migrate from late spring, while dolphins are common year-round and seal-sightings almost guaranteed. See page 77

❹ **Beinn Eighe Nature Reserve** Britain's oldest nature reserve is worth at least an afternoon of exploration. Its 3.5-mile mountain trail wends through Caledonian pine forest to a bleak, otherworldly summit; look out for eagles and wildcats. See page 78

Partly thanks to its proximity to Skye, whose Cuillin range bites into view as you travel south through Wester Ross, this section of the North Coast 500 is particularly popular during the summer months. And deservedly so. The coastal road that wraps from Dundonnell round to Gairloch is one of the most scenic on the North Coast 500, with Highland goats wandering the streets and the almighty An Teallach overseeing proceedings. The sleepy villages of **Poolewe**, **Gairloch** and **Shieldaig** offer gentle and photogenic stop-offs, while the dog-leg road along **Loch Maree** and then back west through **Glen Torridon**, via Kinlochewe, is quite spectacular – with remarkable colour shifts as the sun moves throughout the day. Edge-of-the-world **Applecross** has a lovely pub and a year-round air of excitement, with the ominous **Bealach Na Ba** pass completing the peninsula loop back to **Lochcarron**. From here, the return to **Inverness** is quick, with the landscape levelling out so that the towering hills, single-track passes and sandy bays you've just experienced feel like a distant memory.

GETTING AROUND   WESTER ROSS TO INVERNESS

From Ullapool to Shieldaig, it's a straightforward and scenic **drive**, with a partly single-track road through Glen Torridon west out of Kinlochewe. The main talking point hereabouts is the Applecross Peninsula, and whether or not to attempt the legendary Bealach Na Ba pass. **Large vehicles**, like caravans and camper vans longer than 16ft, or anyone towing a trailer, shouldn't even think about tackling this road, which climbs to 2053ft on a single-track, hairpin road with gradients of twenty percent. If in doubt, turn left at Shieldaig and take the A896, which cuts out the peninsula. **Cyclists** on this leg of the route face a steady incline out of Ullapool before some ups and downs round to Shieldaig. The coastal road round to Applecross is flat; here, the Bealach Na Ba pass poses the most challenging uphill and rewarding downhill of the entire route.

Ullapool to Poolewe

South of Ullapool, the North Coast 500 joins the A832 at **Braemore Junction**, above the head of Loch Broom. Easily accessible from a lay-by on the main road, the spectacular 160ft **Falls of Measach** plunge through the mile-long **Corrieshalloch Gorge**, formed by glacial meltwaters. After walking for five minutes you'll reach a Victorian suspension bridge that spans the chasm, offering a vertiginous view of the falls and gorge, whose 197ft vertical sides are draped in wych elm, goat willow and bird cherry.

It's a great drive from here to Poolewe, along a road that tracks high above Little Loch Broom with gorgeous views to mountains opposite. **Badrallach**, seven miles from a right turn at the head of the loch, is a magical spot to escape for a day or two. The road

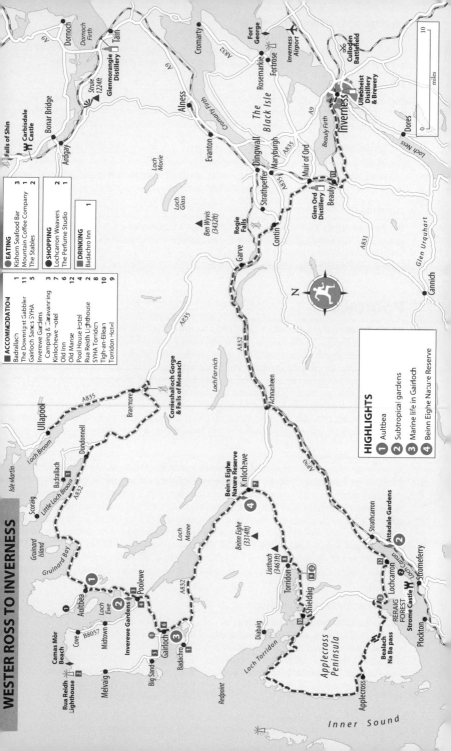

WESTER ROSS TO INVERNESS

HIGHLIGHTS

1 Aultbea
2 Subtropical gardens
3 Marine life in Gairloch
4 Beinn Eighe Nature Reserve

N

5

skirts the shores of **Gruinard Bay**, with fabulous views and some sandy beaches at the inner end of the bay, before reaching the charming fishing village of **Aultbea**.

ACTIVITIES

Ewe Canoe Mellon Charles, Aultbea; https://ewecanoe. co.uk. Explore sheltered sea lochs, wide sandy bays and idyllic lochs surrounded by mountains with this established company. Friendly, qualified and experienced instructors can cater for first-timers as well as experts looking to improve their strokes. From £110 for 1–2 people.

ACCOMMODATION AND EATING   ULLAPOOL TO POOLEWE

Badrallach Croft 9, Badrallach; https://badrallach. com. Views, space and pure escapism literally at the end of the road. There's a campsite, beds in a snug bothy plus B&B in a sweet two-bedroom cottage (week minimum), all with excellent eco-friendly facilities. With fishing rod and kayak rental, too, you can happily settle in here for a few days. £̲

SHOPPING

The Perfume Studio Aultbea; www.perfumestudio scotland.com. Home-made soaps and perfumes, plus tasteful Highlands bric-a-brac are sold at the gift shop. After a browse, settle in at the adjacent *Aroma Café* for a truly stunning perspective across Loch Ewe towards the Torridon mountains – a great spot for a toastie or coffee and cake. Easter–Oct Tues–Sun 10–5pm.

Poolewe

At the sheltered southern end of Loch Ewe is the sleepy village of **POOLEWE**. During World War II, the Arctic convoy embarked from here and the deep-water loch remains one of only three berths for nuclear submarines. One of the area's best **walks** begins nearby, signposted from the lay-by viewpoint on the A832, a mile south. It takes a couple of hours to follow the easy trail across open moorland to the shores of **Loch Maree** (see page 77), then the car park at Slattadale, seven miles southeast of Gairloch. Double-check timetables (01445 712255), but you should be able to continue along the loch shore to catch the Wester bus from Inverness back to Poolewe from the *Loch Maree Hotel* just after 7pm (Tues, Thurs & Fri only).

Inverewe Gardens

Half a mile north of Poolewe on A832 • **Visitor Centre & Restaurant**: April–Oct daily 9.30am–4pm • Charge; NTS • www.nts.org.uk

Most visitors arrive in Poolewe for **Inverewe Gardens**, a subtropical-style oasis of foliage and riotously colourful compared to the wild coast. The gardens were the brainchild of **Osgood MacKenzie** who collected plants from all over the world for his walled garden, which still forms the nucleus of the complex. A network of paths and walkways wanders through more than a dozen gardens featuring exotic plant collections from as far afield as Chile, China, Tasmania and the Himalayas. Mid-May to mid-June is the best time to see the rhododendrons and azaleas, while the herbaceous garden reaches its peak in July and August, as does the wonderful Victorian vegetable and flower garden beside the sea.

ACCOMMODATION AND EATING   POOLEWE

Inverewe Gardens Camping & Caravanning Centre of Poolewe on A832; www.campingandcaravanningclub. co.uk. As trim a site as usual from a member of the Camping & Caravanning Club and largely occupied by motorhomes. Facilities are well maintained and a few pitches in a shady corner allow campers to wake up to loch views. Easter–Oct. £̲

★ **Pool House Hotel** Centre of Poolewe on A832 https://pool-house.co.uk. Once the residence of Inverewe Gardens' Osgood MacKenzie, the Harrison family home remains one of the Highlands' most elegantly opulent small hotels – think rich fabrics, family antiques and art, loch views and a serene sense of calm. Don't be surprised if you struggle to leave the lounge. Easter–Oct. £̲£̲£̲£̲

5 | Gairloch and around

Cheerful and unpretentious, **GAIRLOCH** thrives as a low-key holiday resort, with several sandy beaches for the bucket-and-spade brigade, some good coastal walks within easy reach and an abundance of wildlife cruise operators that pray for passing minke whales. The township is divided into distinct areas spread along Loch Gairloch: to the south, in **Flowerdale Bay**, is Charlestown with the harbour; west, at the turn-off to Melvaig, **Achtercairn** is the centre of Gairloch; and along the north side of the bay is the crofting area of **Strath**. Near the *Old Inn* in Charlestown, the **Sòlas Gallery** (Sept–June Mon–Sat 1–5pm, July & Aug daily 1–5pm; 01445 712626) is worth a stop for its ceramics and watercolours inspired by the Highlands landscapes. A 1.5-mile walk (round trip) tracks the Flowerdale River through a woodland glen to a waterfall.

Gairloch Museum

By the turn-off from the A832 into Achtercairn • April–Oct Wed–Sat 11am–4pm • Charge • www.gairlochmuseum.org

The **Gairloch Heritage Museum** houses eclectic displays of traditional Highland life, from a mock-up crofthouse to one of the largest Fresnel lenses ever constructed, formerly in the nearby Rua Reidh Lighthouse, plus a temporary art exhibition. The archive and library contains a wealth of information on genealogy, local history and Gaelic language (access by appointment). Plans for a change of premises to the Old Anti-aircraft Operations Room in the centre of the village are currently under way, so check ahead.

Big Sand and Melvaig

The area's real attraction is its **coastline**. There's a **beach** just north of the harbour in Charlestown, a crescent of pure sand, or a more impressive stretch a few miles around the north side of the bay at **Big Sand** – it's cleaner, quieter and a mite more pebbly. The B8021 terminates at the crofting hamlet of **Melvaig**, where a community-funded replacement for the legendary but now-closed *Melvaig Inn* is in the pipeline.

Rua Reidh and around

From Melvaig, a private track heads three miles to **Rua Reidh** (pronounced "roo-a-ray"), where a fully operational lighthouse houses a hostel in its keepers' quarters (see page 77). Though the approach road is a public right of way, the owners of the lighthouse have taken steps to restrict access. The topic remains a thorny issue among locals, many of whom will insist you can drive, walk or cycle to the lighthouse.

Around the headland lies beautiful **Camas Mòr** beach, from where a marked footpath tracks inland (southeast) beneath a sheer scarp slope, past a string of lochans and ruined crofts to **MIDTOWN** on the east side of the peninsula, four miles north of Poolewe on the B8057. Allow half a day for the full walk from Melvaig to Poolewe, though be aware that few buses travel back to Gairloch from Poolewe (check times on 01445 712255).

Badachro

On the south side of Loch Gairloch, a single-track lane (built with the Destitution Funds raised during the nineteenth-century potato famine) winds past wooded coves and inlets along the loch to **BADACHRO**, a secluded, former fishing village with a wonderful pub (see page 77).

Redpoint

Beyond Badachro, the road winds five miles further to **REDPOINT**, with beautiful beaches of peach-coloured sand on either side of the headland and great views towards Raasay, Skye and the Western Isles. It also marks the trailhead for the wonderful coast walk to Lower Diabaig. Even if you don't fancy a full-blown hike, follow the footpath a mile or so to find an exquisite **beach** on the south side of the headland.

INFORMATION

GAIRLOCH AND AROUND

Tourist information In the community-run Gale Centre in Achtercairn (Mon–Fri 9.30am–5pm, Sat 10am–4pm, Sun 11am–3pm; https://galeactionforum.co.uk).

ACTIVITIES

Gairloch prides itself on wildlife cruises from its harbour. Orcas and minke whales migrate past from late spring to late summer; porpoise and dolphins are common year-round, and seal-spottings are near enough guaranteed. All operators are located on the harbour at Charlestown.

Gairloch Marine Life Centre & Cruises Charlestown; www.porpoise-gairloch.co.uk. Up to three fun and informative trips (10am, 12.30pm & 3pm, Easter–Oct; from £35pp) a day run by the largest operator, which deploys a mini-sub for underwater pictures and a hydrophone to pick up the underwater sounds. Its visitor centre (Easter–Oct daily 10am–4pm) has displays of local sea life.

Hebridean Whale Cruises Charlestown; www.hebridean-whale-cruises.co.uk. As well as in-shore cruises, Gairloch's longest-established operator runs trips (Easter–Oct; from £65pp) in a high-speed RIB that allows it to reach further offshore into the North Minch and out to the Shiant Isles off Lewis.

ACCOMMODATION, EATING AND DRINKING

BADACHRO

Badachro Inn www.badachroinn.com. Settle onto the terrace with a plate of pork belly or creel-caught langoustine and this pub by the old harbour is as fine a place as you'll find for a sunny afternoon. Inside are real ales, excellent malts and a fire for chill evenings. Look out for otters at dawn and dusk. April–Oct daily noon–midnight, Sun 12.30–11pm; Nov–March Wed–Sun same hours; food served Mon–Fri noon–3pm & 6–9pm, Sat & Sun noon–3pm. £££

GAIRLOCH

Mountain Coffee Company Achtercairn; 01445 712316. Here's an unusual find for a small Highlands town – a relaxed café with a global backpacker vibe. Coffees, mammoth-sized scones and toasted bagels with fresh fillings, plus a good on-site bookshop and rooms upstairs. Easter–Nov daily 9am–6pm. £̄

Old Inn Signposted off A832, Charlestown; https://theoldinn.net. Country character abounds in the rooms of this former coaching inn set off the main road beside the Flowerdale River. Expect pretty patchwork-style quilts or tartan headboards in cosy en-suite rooms. Posh-pub specials such as game casserole, plus beers from the on-site microbrewery, provide the sustenance. March–Nov daily 11am–11pm; food served noon–2.30pm & 5–8.30pm. ££

BIG SAND

Gairloch Sands SYHA On B8021, 2.5 miles west of Gairloch; www.hostellingscotland.org.uk. This former hunting lodge is spectacularly sited above the foreshore, with vast views to Skye from its lounge. It dates back to 1880 and rather shows its age. April to late Sept. £̄

RUA REIDH

Rua Reidh Lighthouse Rua Reidh; https://stayata lighthouse.co.uk. Epic seascapes to the Hebrides in the only lighthouse hostel on Britain's west coast (see page 76), with homely decorative touches and private bathrooms throughout. Breakfasts, packed lunches and dinner available for an additional cost. 2-night minimum stay. Easter–Oct. ££

Loch Maree

Dotted with Caledonian-pine-covered islands, **Loch Maree** is one of the area's scenic highlights, best viewed from the A832 road that drops down to its southeastern tip through Glen Docherty; try to time your journey here in early dawn or dusk, when red

5

deer take over the land. At the southeastern end of the loch, the A896 from Torridon meets the A832 from Achnasheen at small **KINLOCHEWE**, a good base if you're heading into the hills.

Beinn Eighe Nature Reserve

The A832 skirts the southern shore of Loch Maree, passing the **Beinn Eighe Nature Reserve**, Britain's oldest national nature reserve, set up in 1951. Parts of the reserve are forested with Caledonian pine, which once covered the whole country, and it is home to pine martens, wildcats, buzzards and golden eagles. A mile north of Kinlochewe, the **Beinn Eighe Visitor Centre** (Easter–Oct daily 10am–5pm; www.nature.scot, search for Beinn Eighe), on the A832, informs visitors about the rare species and has excellent free leaflets covering several walking trails for all abilities. Two **walks** start from the Coille na Glas-Leitir Trails car park just over a mile north of the visitor centre: a mile-long trail into ancient pine woodland and a more challenging 3.5-mile track into the mountains.

ACCOMMODATION AND EATING   **LOCH MAREE**

Kinlochewe Hotel On A832, centre of village; www. kinlochewehotel.co.uk. A traditional hotel dating back to 1850 with a warm welcome and a fantastic line in regional ales and good-value soups and casseroles. Rooms are comfy enough, though en-suites cost extra. An annexe holds a very basic twelve-bed self-catering bunkhouse, with triple-deck bunks in one room (bedding not included). £–££

Loch Torridon

Loch Torridon marks the northern boundary of the Applecross peninsula. From the water rise the mountains of **Liathach** (3461ft) and **Beinn Eighe** (3314ft), shapely hulks of reddish, 750-million-year-old white quartzite. Around fifteen thousand acres of the massif are under the protection of the National Trust for Scotland, which makes this superb walking country, with a trio of Munros to bag.

Torridon

TORRIDON village, at the east end of the loch, marks where the road heads west towards the Applecross Peninsula. The village itself – thirty or so houses and a shop – straggles along the loch beneath the mountains, making it a fine launchpad for hikes. A **Countryside Centre** (Mon–Sat 10am–5pm; donation requested; NTS; www.nts.org.uk/visit/places/torridon) at the turning into the village provides advice on mountain walks plus information on geology, flora and fauna. Their Deer Museum down the road (same hours; free) has information on the history and management of red deer, which are abundant in the region.

Shieldaig

Smuggled off the main road on the shore of Loch Torridon, pretty **SHIELDAIG** ("herring bay") is a gentle spot – until the Shieldaig Fete and Rowing Regatta livens things up with some wacky boat races over the first weekend in August. A track winding north up the peninsula from the village makes for an enjoyable stroll. Otherwise, simply enjoy the view to **Shieldaig Island**, managed by the National Trust for Scotland.

ACTIVITIES   **LOCH TORRIDON**

Torridon Outdoors 1.5 miles southwest of turn-off into   Torridon;   www.thetorridon.com/torridon-outdoors.

A PASSING PLACE ON A WINDING SINGLE TRACK ROAD ON APPLECROSS PENINSULA

5

Based at the historic *Torridon Hotel* (see below), this operator provides a full range of local activities: guided walks, gorge scrambling, coasteering and climbing, plus kayaking, archery and even clay-pigeon shooting. They also hire out mountain bikes, e-bikes and wetsuits for wild swimming. See website for prices.

ACCOMMODATION AND EATING

SHIELDAIG

★ **Tigh-an-Eilean** On the waterfront; http://tighan eilean.co.uk. Faultless service and utter relaxation in a lovely small hotel on the waterfront with classy country accommodation plus a sensational restaurant (reservations essential); expect the likes of west coast sea bream on innovative daily menus. The attached *Shieldaig Bar and Coastal Kitchen* rustles up top-notch bistro dishes like its famous seafood stew and wood-fired pizzas. Bar Feb–New Year daily 11am–11pm; food served March–Oct daily 6–9pm. **££**

TORRIDON

The Stables Next to The Torridon hotel, http://the torridon.com/the-stables. More cyclist- and walker-friendly than the neighbouring *Torridon* (same owners), with neat, modern en-suites. The bar serves regional ales and good gastropub cooking – veggie stir-fry, fish and chips or steak-and-ale pie and there's also a casual restaurant, *Bo & Muc*. Stay in Feb and March for the best value. Feb–Easter Mon–Sat 8am–9pm, Sun till 5pm; Easter–Dec daily 8am–9pm. **£££**

SYHA Torridon Start of village, 100yds from turn-off; http://hostellingscotland.org.uk. Though the 1970s-vintage municipal building is no looker, this hostel is spacious and a popular choice with hikers and bikers thanks to its location beneath the peaks. Provides the usual kitchen, laundry and drying room, plus very cheap meals daily. Closed three weeks in Jan. **£**

★ **The Torridon** 1.5 miles southwest of turn-off into Torridon, https://www.thetorridon.com/stay/the-stables. This Victorian hunting lodge is one of the west coast's grandest stays. Sympathetically styled with boutique-meets-baronial decor in the public areas and Master rooms; classic rooms are more up to date, while the 1887 Suite is pure indulgence. The fine-dining restaurant is splendidly elegant with its daily menus of seasonal modern European cuisine, and the whisky bar with its 350-plus malts is a delight (tasting sessions available). **££££**

Loch Carron

South of the Applecross Peninsula are the twin sea lochs of **Loch Kishorn**, so deep it was once used as an oil-rig construction site, and **Loch Carron**, which cuts far inland to **STRATHCARRON**, a useful rail link between Torridon and Kyle of Lochalsh, but little else.

Lochcarron

With supermarkets, cafés, a bank and fuel set along a long whitewashed seafront, **LOCHCARRON** represents a considerable hub hereabouts. While it's of more use than interest, two crafty sights warrant a browse. A mile north of town on the main road, the **Smithy Community Hub**, a nineteenth-century smithy and forge, has become a focus for local **crafts collectives** selling their wares.

Attadale Gardens

2.5 miles south of Strathcarron • Easter to mid-Oct Mon–Sat 10am–5pm • Charge • http://attadalegardens.com

Made up of twenty artistically landscaped acres, **Attadale Gardens** are ranked among Scotland's finest by horticultural aficionados. Fans include the Duke and Duchess of Rothesay (the titles given to Prince Charles and Camilla while on Scottish duties), who paid a royal visit in June 2016 to view the gardens' waterfalls, Monet bridges and rhododendrons.

INFORMATION AND ACTIVITIES   **LOCH CARRON**

Tourist information Tourist information desk in the Smithy Community Hub (April–May & Sept–Oct Mon–Sat 10am–4pm, June–Aug 10am–5pm; 01520 722952).

Reraig Forest Argo Tours Reraig Forest, https://reraig forest.co.uk. A unique chance to get up close to the resident deer herd, in a bone-rattling all-terrain vehicle (4-person minimum, from £48pp/3hr). Guide Colin brings the history of the area to life with his witty tales. Great for kids. Colin arranges pick-up from Lochcarron; booking essential.

ACCOMMODATION AND EATING

Kishorn Seafood Bar Kishorn, 6 miles northwest of Lochcarron, http://kishornseafoodbar.co.uk. A baby-blue, lodge-like café often named in the top-ten British seafood restaurants for fresh local seafood. Come for sharing platters, Skye mussels or just garlic scallops and a croissant. Outdoor seating available. Easter to mid-July & mid-Sept to Nov Sat–Thurs 10am–5pm, Fri 10am–9pm; mid-July to mid-Sept Mon–Sat 10am–9pm, Sun 10am–5pm. **££**

Old Manse Church St, Lochcarron, http://theoldmanse lochcarron.com. Floral fabrics, pine furniture and wrought-iron beds – country style rules in the five spacious en-suite rooms of the *Old Manse*, on the road to Strome Castle. Perhaps its real appeal is the location before the loch – pay a little extra for a room with a view. **££**

SHOPPING

Lochcarron Weavers 2 miles south of Lochcarron towards Strome Castle, http://lochcarron.co.uk. One of Scotland's leading manufacturers of tartan. Drop by this workshop to see weaving demonstrations, and buy fabrics and clothing. Easter–Oct Mon–Sat 9am–5pm, Nov–Easter Mon–Fri 10am–4pm.

The road to Inverness

After the hundreds of miles it took to travel from Inverness to Wester Ross, via craggy coastlines and white-knuckle mountain passes, there's something a bit anticlimactic about the speedy return from Lochcarron to the east coast. If you didn't manage to catch them on your departure from Inverness when you first set off, be sure to stop by Rogie Falls (see page 39) and have a cuppa in Strathpeffer (see page 38) before crossing the finish line of the North Coast 500 in Inverness. The cute town of **Beauly** (a transliteration of "beau lieu", meaning "beautiful place") is also worth a stop-off; the ruins of the Beauly Priory are set in pretty grounds, and The Square has a line of quaint gift shops and cafés. Swing by Corner on the Square, High St, (https://www. corneronthesquare.co) for excellent coffee, a great deli, and a selection of local groceries to take home. In January 2023, an 800-year-old wych elm tree believed to be Europe's oldest sadly fell down in Beauly Priory.

ACCOMMODATION AND EATING

★ **The Downright Gabbler** Beauly, https://downright gabbler.co.uk. An 1830s former coaching inn completely transformed as an intimate, immersive dining experience with exceptionally good value self-catering apartments above. Daring set menus are complemented by stories of Scotland's most famous storytellers, its best drams, and more. A truly unique experience. Afternoon tea and bespoke dinner themes available; contact well ahead. Year-round; Food events Fri, Sat or Sun, 2pm or 7pm start **££** Apartments **£**

Small print and index

A ROUGH GUIDE TO ROUGH GUIDES

Published in 1982, the first Rough Guide – to Greece – was a student scheme that became a publishing phenomenon. Mark Ellingham, a recent graduate in English from Bristol University, had been travelling in Greece the previous summer and couldn't find the right guidebook. With a small group of friends he wrote his own guide, combining a contemporary, journalistic style with a thoroughly practical approach to travellers' needs.

The immediate success of the book spawned a series that rapidly covered dozens of destinations. And, in addition to impecunious backpackers, Rough Guides soon acquired a much broader readership that relished the guides' wit and inquisitiveness as much as their enthusiastic, critical approach and value-for-money ethos. These days, Rough Guides include recommendations from budget to luxury and cover more than 120 destinations around the globe, from Amsterdam to Zanzibar, all regularly updated by our team of roaming writers.

Browse all our latest guides, read inspirational features and book your trip at **roughguides.com**.

Rough Guide credits

Updater: Richard Franks
Editors: Annie Warren, Rachel Lawrence
Cartography: Katie Bennett
Picture editor: Tom Smyth

Layout: Pradeep Thapliyal
Head of DTP and Pre-Press: Rebeka Davies
Head of Publishing: Sarah Clark

Publishing information

Third Edition 2023

Distribution

UK, Ireland and Europe
Apa Publications (UK) Ltd; sales@roughguides.com
United States and Canada
Ingram Publisher Services; ips@ingramcontent.com
Australia and New Zealand
Booktopia; retailer@booktopia.com.au
Worldwide
Apa Publications (UK) Ltd; sales@roughguides.com

Special Sales, Content Licensing and CoPublishing
Rough Guides can be purchased in bulk quantities
at discounted prices. We can create special editions,
personalised jackets and corporate imprints tailored to
your needs. sales@roughguides.com.
roughguides.com

Printed in Turkey

Contains Ordnance Survey data © Crown copyright and
database rights 2023

This book was produced using **Typefi** automated
publishing software.

A catalogue record for this book is available from the
British Library

The publishers and authors have done their best to
ensure the accuracy and currency of all the information
in **The Rough Guide to North Coast 500**, however,
they can accept no responsibility for any loss, injury, or
inconvenience sustained by any traveller as a result of
information or advice contained in the guide.

Help us update

We've gone to a lot of effort to ensure that this edition of
The Rough Guide to North Coast 500 is accurate and up-
to-date. However, things change – places get "discovered",
opening hours are notoriously fickle, restaurants and
rooms raise prices or lower standards. If you feel we've got
it wrong or left something out, we'd like to know, and if
you can remember the address, the price, the hours, the
phone number, so much the better.

Please send your comments with the subject line
"Rough Guide North Coast 500 Update" to mail@
uk.roughguides.com. We'll credit all contributions and
send a copy of the next edition (or any other Rough Guide
if you prefer) for the very best emails.

Acknowledgements

This guide was created in partnership with **North Coast 500 Limited**

Photo credits

(Key: T-top; C-centre; B-bottom; L-left; R-right)

Alamy 8, 9C, 11T, 11B, 15, 30, 37, 59, 71, 79
Getty Images 10B

Shutterstock 1, 2, 4, 5, 9TL, 9TR, 9B, 10T, 10C, 12, 13, 20, 47, 50, 55, 65, 75

Cover: Highland bull on the road **Tom Jastram/Shutterstock**

Index